1000 GLASS BEADS

Innovation & Imagination in Contemporary Glass Beadmaking

1000 GLASS BEADS

Innovation & Imagination in Contemporary Glass Beadmaking

Introduction by Cathy Finegan

LARK BOOKS

A Division of Sterling Publishing Co., Inc.
New York

Editor: Valerie Van Arsdale Shrader
Art Director: Stacey Budge
Cover Designer: Barbara Zaretsky
Associate Art Director:
Shannon Yokeley
Editorial Assistance: Delores Gosnell,
Jeff Hamilton, Anne Wolff Hollyfield,
Rebecca Lim, Nathalie Mornu
Art Interns: Laura Gabris,
Evan Krokowski

Cover Images: Front, Kristina Logan,
Collection of Beads, 2003, photo by
Paul Avis; Back (top), Harlan Simon,
Three Beads, 2002, photo by Richard
Reed, Rich Images; Back (bottom
left), Wayne Robbins, *Frog on a Leaf
Bead,* 2002, photo by Paul Avis; Back
(bottom right), Sara Hoyt, *Lush,* 2003,
photo by artist; Spine, Ver et
Framboise (Nicole Zumkeller and Eric
Seydoux), *Various Beads and
Cabochons,* 2001, photo by artist;
Front flap, Kristina Logan, *Three Ivory
Totem Beads,* 2003, photo by Paul
Avis; Back flap, Sylvus Tarn, *Triple
Hollow Beads,* 2003, photo by artist

Interior Images: Title page (left),
Amy Haftkowycz, *Assorted
Borosilicate Beads,* 2003, photo by
Steven Waskow; Title page (right),
Linda MacMillan, *Collection,* 2002,
photo by R. Diamante, Portland,
Maine; Contents, Daniel Adams,
Offset Eye Beads, 2002, photo by
Roger Schreiber

Library of Congress Cataloging-in-Publication Data

Shrader, Valerie Van Arsdale.
  1000 glass beads : innovation & imagination in
contemporary glass beadmaking / Valerie Van Arsdale Shrader ; introduction by Cathy Finegan.
    p. cm.
Includes index.
  ISBN 1-57990-458-0 (pbk.)
  1. Glass beads—Catalogs. 2. Beadwork—Catalogs. I. Title:

    One thousand glass beads. II. Title.
NK5440.B34S55 2004
748.8'5—dc22

                          2003022534

10 9 8 7 6 5 4 3

Published by Lark Books, a division of
Sterling Publishing Co., Inc.
387 Park Avenue South, New York, N.Y. 10016

© 2004, Lark Books

Distributed in Canada by Sterling Publishing,
c/o Canadian Manda Group, 165 Dufferin Street
Toronto, Ontario, Canada M6K 3H6

Distributed in the U.K. by Guild of Master Craftsman Publications Ltd.,
Castle Place, 166 High Street, Lewes, East Sussex, England
BN7 1XU
Tel: (+ 44) 1273 477374, Fax: (+ 44) 1273 478606,
Email: pubs@thegmcgroup.com, Web: www.gmcpublications.com

Distributed in Australia by Capricorn Link (Australia) Pty Ltd.,
P.O. Box 704, Windsor, NSW 2756 Australia

If you have questions or comments about this book, please contact:
Lark Books
67 Broadway
Asheville, NC 28801
(828) 253-0467

Manufactured in China

ISBN 1-57990-458-0

CONTENTS

INTRODUCTION

Beads have been with us for a very long time; the earliest ones, dating back some 40,000 years ago, were made of animal bones and teeth. But glass beads—born of flame and fancy—began to appear around 4,000 years ago. Not too long afterward, glass beads were considered as valuable as precious stones, worn primarily by nobility. Later, they were used as currency.

The Venetians, who mastered the art of glass beadmaking, guarded their secrets with great ferocity; the beadmakers sequestered on the island of Murano were threatened with death if they disclosed how they made glass beads. Inevitably, of course, their techniques leaked out to the rest of the world. Now, this fascination with fire and glass has become one of the most exciting contemporary art forms, its boundaries constantly being explored by innovative artists on every continent.

Why? The material itself has a special allure: glass can be transparent or opaque, shiny or dull, multi-colored or colorless. It is both strong and fragile, forgiving and temperamental, utilitarian and frivolous. But the process of glass beadmaking involves more than the raw material. There is also the mystery of the flame: too much or too little oxygen affects the appearance of the bead. So it is the artist's skill that makes a bead from glass and flame, with the beadmaker acting as a choreographer, encouraging the dance between the elements. Like any other artistic endeavor, it is a process of intention, patience, discovery, surprise, and hope. The cold glass rod must be introduced slowly in the flame, or it will shatter. Once warm, the artist begins to manipulate the molten glass, its consistency like honey, caressing it into the desired shape. Because the final color isn't apparent when the glass is molten, the beauty of the bead is not revealed until it is removed from the annealing kiln. Sometimes the bead is exactly as hoped; other times, something completely unexpected—perhaps even magical—may have occurred.

Modern-day practitioners of the art of glass beadmaking describe their work in various ways—as an obsession, as a passion, but almost always as a partnership with the torch. Some even speak of it as a meditation, as they become entranced by the mesmerizing qualities of the molten glass and the flame. The contemporary glass bead movement is in fact a fairly recent phenomenon, begun in the early 1970s. A handful of artists, who had been working in virtual anonymity, gathered in 1993 in conjunction with an exhibit of modern glass beads sponsored by the Bead Museum in Prescott, Arizona. The Society of Glass Beadmakers (SGB), now known as the International Society of Glass Beadmakers (ISGB), emerged from this meeting with a mission to preserve the history of glass beadmaking and promote education about the art form. The ISGB and other related groups help inspire contemporary beadmakers and provide a nurturing atmosphere for creativity.

The artists of today use a number of techniques to create engaging artwork from the pas de deux of flame and glass. Lampworking, also called flameworking, is the most common method, where glass is melted in the heat of a torch and wound around a steel mandrel.

Bronwen Heilman, *Escape From the Gated Community*, 2002. Photo by Robin Stancliff

In kilnforming, or fusing, layers of glass, metals, and inclusions are melted together in a kiln; in kilncasting, shards of glass are placed in a mold and fired in a kiln. Glass blowers can make beads as well. Glass tubing is also being used in beadmaking, with the decorating being done on the inside of the tube rather than on the outside, producing an intriguing bead with a totally different look.

And there are now artists who combine these techniques, with studios all over the world literally glowing with creativity. Individual artistic expression and experimentation abounds. Some examples: Tom Holland creates contemporary interpretations of historical beads; Leah Fairbanks and Kristen Franzen Orr craft incredibly detailed floral beads; and Wayne Robbins makes amazing sculptural beads in borosilicate glass.

Kim Miles, *Daffodils,* 2003. Photo by artist

There are whimsical masterpieces by Sharon Peters, and there are artists whose work exhibits exacting precision and geometric perfection, including Lani Ching, Terrl Caspary Schmidt, and Emiko Sawamoto. There are beads created in the furnace by Ralph Mossman and Mary Mullaney, and in the kiln by Candy Beth Michalski and Karen Kay Velarde. Beau Anderson and Lauri Copeland coldwork their beads, adding the lapidary's skill to their pieces made in the flame. Glass is being worked with metals by René Roberts, electroformed by Kate Fowle Meleney, sandblasted by Diana East, and painted by Bronwen Heilman. Look at the beads created by these artists and you will be astonished by their originality and execution.

These highly skilled practitioners have transformed the bead from currency to high art. Glass beadmaking is recognized in museums throughout the world, and beads are sought after by both glass and bead collectors. The beads being made today demonstrate such skill and individual flair I expect they will be collected for many years, and then cherished for generations to come as miniature works of art.

Explore the achievements of these artists as you leaf through this book, for there is no better place to experience the alchemy that produces the glass bead. These selections, hundreds of images from the world over, showcase the creative abilities and personalities of each beadmaker. Their beads are both fine art and functional, wearable and collectible, simple and complex, forthright and mysterious. They have been created by some of the most recognized glass bead artists working today, as well as those whose talents have yet to be discovered. I hope this book opens your eyes to what is possible through the choreography of glass, fire, and imagination.

Cathy Finegan

SGB Past President (1999-2001)
ISGB Past President (2001-2002)

Susan Breen Silvy, *Enameled States Keum Boo Series,* 2003. Photo by Jeff O'Dell

Patti L. Cahill, *Spirograph Button (Swimsuit),* 2003. Photo by artist

SANDY LENT
Geometric Beads, 2003

Lampworked; layered dots; stringer; dichroic and soda-lime glass

1.25 x 1 x 1.25 cm (each bead)

Photo by Tom Lent

AMY WALDMAN ENGEL
Silver Granite, 2003

Lampworked; silver foil; soda-lime glass

4 x 1.2 x 1.2 cm

Photo by artist

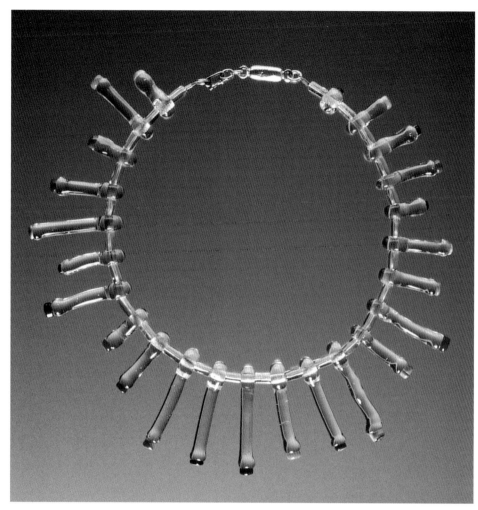

The inspiration for my design comes mainly from my exploration of glass itself. My work is described as surprisingly modern *and* primitive.

JULIA SKOP
Secret Surprise, 2002

Flameworked; millefiore; soda-lime glass; metal clay clasp and sterling catch

45.7 cm (necklace); 3.8 cm (largest bead)

Photo by Chris Bretschneider

PATTI DOUGHERTY
Marine Life Beads, 2003

Lampworked; pearlescent enamel; soda-lime glass

Dimensions vary

Photo by Peter Groesbeck

STEPHANIE SERSICH
Necklace of Handmade Beads, 2002

Lampworked; plunged and encased dots;
soda-lime glass; sterling findings

50.8 cm (necklace)

Photo by R. Diamante, Portland, Maine

11

CHRISTINA BAKER
Venus Bag, 2002

Lampworked; etched; soda-lime glass

75 cm (strap); 10 x 15 cm (pouch)

Photo by Jerry Anthony Photography

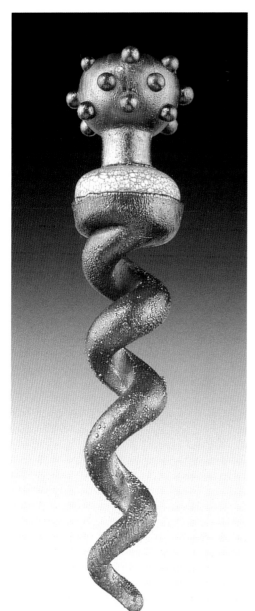

SUSAN BREEN SILVY
Enameled States Keum Boo Series, 2003

Lampworked; enamel overlay; soda-lime glass;
depletion-gilded sterling silver tubing with
24k gold interior (Keum Boo technique)

4.8 x 2.2 cm

Photo by Jeff O'Dell

KATE FOWLE MELENEY
Spiral Anthropomorph, 2002

Lampworked; fumed; patinaed copper
electroforming; soda-lime glass

11.4 x 1.6 cm

Photo by Jerry Anthony Photography

13

Garber's

assorted chocolates

Assortment of fine handmade glass chocolates.
Ingredients: made from imported Italian glass. No calories.

ERNA GARBER
Chocolate Beads, 2002

Lampworked; stringer; soda-lime glass

2.5 x 1.9 cm (each bead)

Photo by Bronwen Sexton

Melting glass is so darned much fun, and I really like working bright colors into elaborate shapes. When I'm done with work I have to do, I mess around with these faces, trying to add specific personality quirks—so far I've got three of the seven deadly sins, but I can't make them stop smiling!

SHARON PETERS
Ghouls Just Wanna Have Fun, 2003

Lampworked; sculpted; four-part compound bead; twistie; enamel stringer; ribbon cane; trapped air bubbles; tea staining; soda-lime glass

8.3 x 6.4 x 5 cm

Photo by Janice Peacock

15

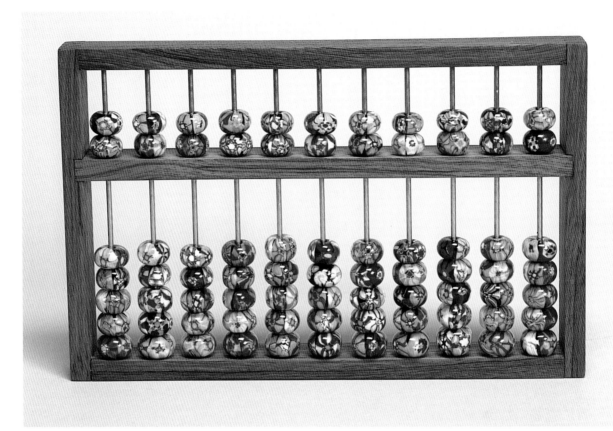

A Venetian paperweight that I saw at age five burned its image in my memory. My millefiore canes and beads are homage to that paperweight and connection to the wonderment I felt.

CONNIE POLLARD
Abacus: Beads Count, 2003

Lampworked; encased; original millefiore; soda-lime glass; stainless steel rods

Teak frame by John Keller Pollard

14.9 x 23.8 x 2.9 cm (frame); 1 x 1.6 cm (beads)

Photo by Susan Byrne Photography

STEPHANIE SERSICH
Pod-Blossom Bead, 2003

Lampworked; stacked dots; soda-lime glass

3.8 x 3.8 x 3.8 cm

Photo by R. Diamante, Portland, Maine

ELLIE BURKE
Blown Reversal Hot Dog Bead, 2002

Flameworked; blown; reverse twist;
borosilicate glass tubing; sterling
silver cable

6.4 x 1.9 x 1.9 cm

Photo by Lawrence Sanders

DEBBY WEAVER
Wild Woman Pendant with Stand, 2002

Lampworked, soda-lime glass; low-fired ceramic stand with steel rods

15.2 x 10.2 x 7.6 cm (stand); 8.9 cm (pendant)

Photo by Theodore R. Wailes

JILL A. SYMONS
Blueberry Set, 2002

Lampworked; stringer;
soda-lime glass

21.5 cm (necklace);
15 mm (largest bead)

Photo by artist

This style has for me long been
a signature look; steady lines
and smooth swirls that have
not been fully melted flat.

19

DEANNA GRIFFIN DOVE
Margo (Kaleidoscope Series), 2002

Flameworked; raked, stacked dots; soda-lime glass

1.9 x 3.8 x 1.9 cm

Photo by artist

In my search for luscious color combinations, I often try to figure out what colors someone else would choose—as a way of breaking habits. Margo Knight, one of my students, influenced these colors.

SANDRA SAYLOR SEAMAN
Earth Abstract Tab, 2003

Lampworked; enamel powder; silver foil; goldstone; soda-lime glass

25 x 20 x 7 mm

Photo by artist

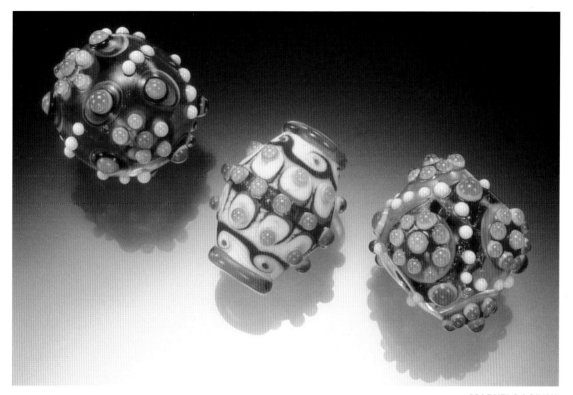

MARKELS LORINI
3 Beads (Dots Chinese Style), 2003

Flameworked; masking techniques; stacked dots; acid
etched; dichroic and soda-lime glass

2.5 x 3.2 x 3.2 cm (largest bead)

Photo by Ralph Gabriner

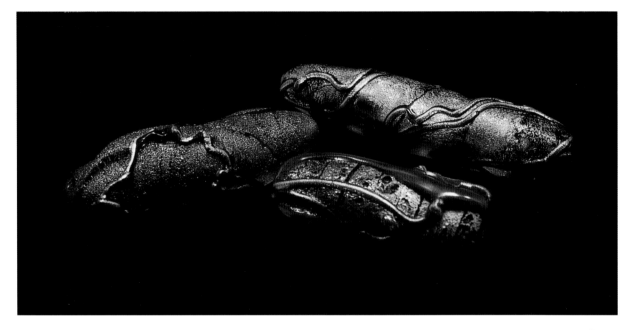

CAY DICKEY
Loose Beads, 2002

Flameworked; stringer; dichroic and soda-lime glass

7.6 x 1.3 cm

Photo by Carl Tamura

LINDA MACMILLAN
Collection, 2002

Lampworked; dichroic and soda-lime glass

2.5 x 1.9 x .6 cm (largest bead)

Photo by R. Diamante, Portland, Maine

For me, the art and craft of glass beadmaking is about freezing a small piece of time, light, and motion into a tangible form that can be worn and passed from hand to hand for generations to come.

KIM MILES
Woven Floral Tab, 2003

Lampworked; tabular; layered; plunged; heavily encased; soda-lime glass

4.3 x 3.5 x 1.6 cm

Photo by artist

LORI ENGLE
Beads of a Feather, 2000

Lampworked; soda-lime glass; handcarved mahogany base, with peacock feather encased in glass and 14k-gold bead and crystal accents

Base by Paul Engle

22.9 x 15.2 x 25.4 cm (mobile)

Photo by Paul Engle

BARBARA A. WRIGHT
Lampworked Glass Bead Necklace, 1999

Lampworked; soda-lime glass; red horn and silver accents with hand-made sterling silver chain

55 cm (necklace)

Photo by Hap Sakwa

It's all about color and shape. I find the richer and more vibrant the colors I work with, the more inspired my carved designs become. I work in a very spontaneous and freeform way and allow the glass and its colors to guide my hands.

TERI SOKOLOFF
Visions, 2003

Kilnformed; carved; dichroic and fusible glass; waxed linen cord and silver beads

7.6 x 2.5 cm

Photo by S. Sokoloff

27

I like to do work that makes me smile
and challenges my skills at the same time.

WAYNE ROBBINS
Peeking Frog Necklace, 2001

Lampworked; sculpted; fused; surface decoration of frit
and gold leaf; borosilicate glass

5.4 x 5.7 x 4.4 cm

Photo by Tony Grant

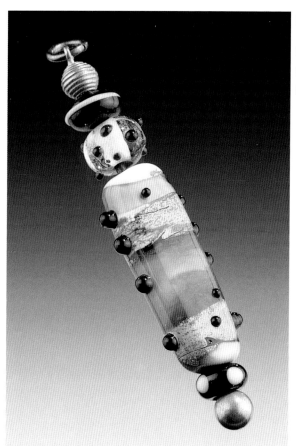

BARBARA K. HOLLOSY
Pink with Silver Foil Series, 2001

Lampworked; silver foil; stringers; soda-lime glass

5.7 cm

Photo by Jerry Anthony Photography

GAIL BOO
Help Me, 2002

Lampworked; soda-lime glass;
electroformed pendant

5 x 3.8 x 1.3 cm

Photo by Linda LoPresti

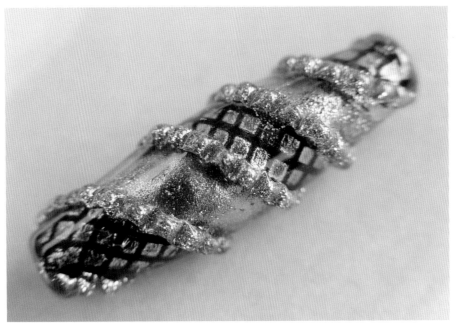

PATRICIA A. FRANTZ
Dichroic and Goldstone Spiral, 2003

Lampworked; bicone; raised spiral goldstone
decoration; dichroic and soda-lime glass

1.3 x 3.8 cm

Photo by artist

EMIKO SAWAMOTO
Gold Fabergé Egg, 2003

Lampworked; gold foil; cubic zirconia; lead and
soda-lime glass

3 x 2.3 cm

Photo by Rich Images

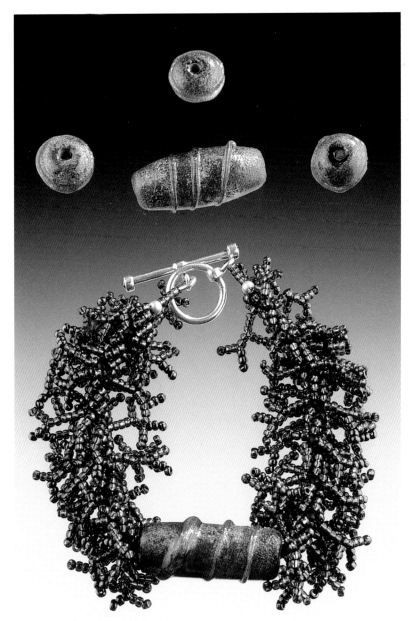

CHRISTINA BAKER
Fringe with Handmade Beads, 2002

Lampworked; layered enamel powder; gold-stone stringer; soda-lime glass

20 cm (bracelet)

Photo by Jerry Anthony Photography

In addition to these ornament beads, my species-specific hummingbird pendants are especially designed for comfort, flattened to lie against the wearer's body and balanced to hang correctly.

PATRICIA STOLL
Ruby-Throated Hummingbird, 2003

Lampworked; sculpted; off-hand technique; dichroic and soda-lime glass

3.6 x 2.5 x 2 cm

Photo by David Orr

KIM MILES
Orango CZ Flowers, 2003

Lampworked; plunged floral; heavily encased;
cubic zirconia, soda-lime glass

2.4 x 2.8 x 2.8 cm

Photo by artist

KIM MILES
Daffodils, 2003

Lampworked; plunged floral; heavily encased;
soda-lime glass

2.2 x 2.9 x 2.9 cm

Photo by artist

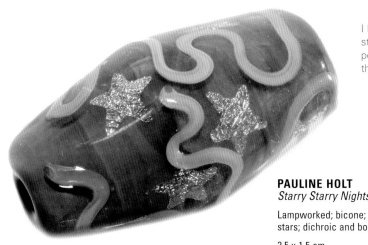

I have always been fascinated by stars. I have worked long and hard to perfect a dichroic star technique—I think this works.

PAULINE HOLT
Starry Starry Nights, 2003

Lampworked; bicone; encased; stringer; fused stars; dichroic and borosilicate glass

2.5 x 1.5 cm

Photo by artist

HEATHER TRIMLETT
Hollow-Formed Beads, 2003

Lampworked; hollow; molded; raised dots; two-color twist; soda-lime glass

3.2 x 1.3 cm (largest bead)

Photo by Melinda Holden

DEB RYMAN
Red Heart with Silver Dots, 2002

Lampworked; formed; fine silver;
soda-lime glass

3.75 x 2.5 x 1.9 cm

Photo by Jerry Anthony Photography

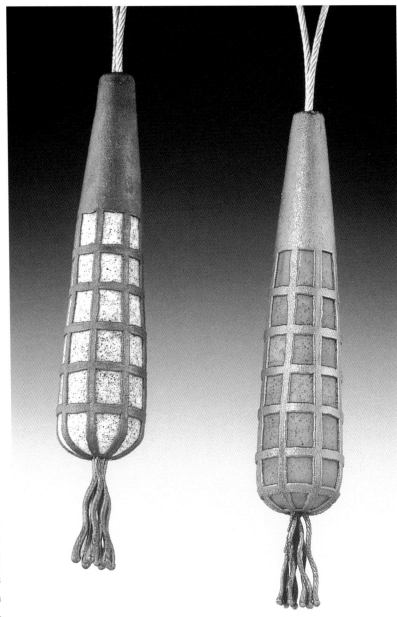

KATE FOWLE MELENEY
Yurts, 2003

Lampworked; sifted enamel;
electroformed copper with
patina; soda-lime glass

9.5 x 1.9 cm

Photo by Jerry Anthony Photography

DANIEL ADAMS
Echinoidea, 2003

Lampworked; trail decoration; engraved enamels;
frit; reduction frit; dots; soda-lime glass

83.8 (necklace); 5.7 x 1.6 x 1.6 cm (largest bead)

Photo by Roger Schreiber

LISAJOY SACHS
Tree of Life, 2002

Lampworked; soda-lime glass; sterling
silver; reversible pendant

6.4 x 3.2 x 2.2 cm

Photo by Keith Meiser

ELIZABETH RYLAND MEARS
Out My Winter Window V, 2002

Flameworked; blown; sandblasted; borosilicate glass;
silver cable, industrial tubing, and grommets

30.5 x 40.6 x 10.2 cm (box)

Photo by Tommy Olof Elder

Living in the mountains of Colorado inspires me to create vignettes of nature.

GINNY SYCURO
Sign of Autumn, 2003

Lampworked; color applied in reverse; borosilicate glass

6.4 x 3.2 x 1.3 cm

Photo by Azad

DANIEL ADAMS
Grey Sampler, 2003

Lampworked; encased; dots;
combed and feathered; engraved
enamels; frit; trail decoration; silver inclusions; soda-lime glass

Polymer clay beads
by Cynthia Toops

55 cm (necklace); 3.2 x 3.2 x 2.5 cm
(largest bead)

Photo by Roger Schreiber

WAYNE ROBBINS
Deep Sea Angler, 2002

Lampworked; sculpted; fused; frit; borosilicate glass; twisted square silver stock

2.5 x 3.8 x 1.9 cm

Photo by Paul Avis

ALLISON LINDQUIST
Deep Space, 2001

Flameworked; layered; stringer; cane; latticino; metal burnout; enamel; soda-lime glass

5 x 1.9 cm

Photo by Don Tuttle

KATHLEEN DENNISON
Transformation, 2002

Lampworked; hollow; goldstone and silver
stringer; palladium leaf; dichroic and soda-lime
glass; woven sterling silver and 14k gold
neckpiece (hollow construction)

45.7 x 1.3 x 5 cm (neckpiece); 2.5 x 1.9 cm (beads)

Photo by Ralph Gabriner

SUSAN BREEN SILVY
Brocade, 2002

Lampworked; carved reduction design; fine silver overlay; soda-lime glass; sterling silver tubing riveted through center

4.1 x 2.5 x 3.2 cm

Photo by Jerry Anthony Photography

CONSTANCE PAULDING
Flower Beads, 2002

Flameworked; plunged dots; filigrana; soda-lime glass

2.5 cm (largest bead)

Photo by Jeff Baird

DEB RYMAN
Babaluo Beads, 2002

Lampworked; shaped; stringer; iridized; soda lime glass

4.4 x 1.6 x 1.9 cm (largest bead)

Photo by Jerry Anthony Photography

CONNIE POLLARD
Five Buttons, 2003

Lampworked; on-mandrel with glass shanks; original murrini; soda-lime glass

1.6 to 1.9 cm

Photo by Susan Byrne Photography

Lampwork has become my passion
as a form of artistic expression. I can
incorporate color exploration, form, beauty,
and whimsy all in one.

OFILIA J. CINTA
Hollow Lampwork Fish Beads, 2002

Lampworked; hollow; aventurine; dichroic and soda-lime glass

7.5 x 6.3 x 3.8 cm (largest bead)

Photo by Rich Images

JEANINE L. OWEN
Cirque D' Chat (Circus of Cats), 2003

Lampworked; original stringer, ribbon, and
latticino cane; soda-lime glass

2.5 x 2.5 cm

Photo by artist

Sometimes while working
at the torch I play with
new ideas. A jointed teddy
bear caught my fancy.

GINNY SYCURO
Teddy, 2002

Lampworked; articulated limbs
(separate beads); soda-lime glass

5 x 3.2 x 2.5 cm

Photo by Jerry Downs

47

This piece came from a series of figures that were intended to be spontaneous. For instance, this one was made while listening to a James Brown CD.

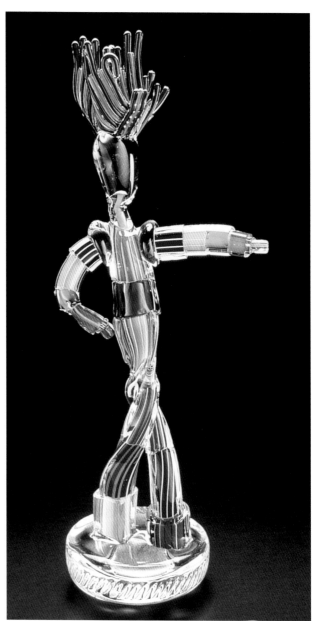

MICHAEL SCHMIDT
"I Feel Good…," 2000

Hand-drawn; cut; fused; picked up hot and worked off-hand; soda-lime glass

45.7 x 17.8 x 12.7 cm

Photo by Charles Frizzel

BETH WILLIAMS
Black Leaves Necklace, 2002

Lampworked; layered; shaped; gold leaf; dichroic and soda-lime glass; handforged sterling silver links, handmade fine silver cable

40.6 cm (necklace); 2.5 x 1.7 x .6 cm (beads)

Photo by Steve Gyurina

My wacky sense of humor comes out with the bright, happy colors I always use, and in the frogs, lizards, and other creatures I create.

ASHLEY WATSON
Two Sides of Every Story Pendant, 2003

Lampworked; stringer; dots; flattened and snipped; soda-lime glass; sterling silver findings

1 x .5 x .5 cm

Photo by Josh Phillips

SHARON PETERS
Nuclear Fishin', 2002

Lampworked; heat and gravity shaped; textured; etched; applied dichroic coating; soda-lime glass

3.8 x 5.7 x 2.5 cm (each bead)

Photo by Janice Peacock

PAMELA KAY WOLFERSBERGER
Primarily Vessels Series, 2002

Lampworked; soda-lime glass; black onyx, sterling, moonstone, crystal, and peridot accents

61 cm (necklace)

Photo by Jerry Anthony Photography

BRUCE ST. JOHN MAHER
Bull's-Eyes, 2002

Heat laminated; coldworked;
dichroic glass

Dimensions vary

Photo by Robert K. Liu

There is magic
in melting glass,
and I believe I have
found it. Or, has it
found me?

DOLLY AHLES
Cosmic Storm, 2003

Lampworked; encased; layered;
twisted stringer; silver foil and
wire; soda-lime glass

3.8 x 2.5 cm

Photo by Jeff Scovil

CAROL BUGARIN
Untitled, 2002

Lampworked; iridized; soda-lime
glass; silver links

50.8 cm (necklace); 2.5 cm (disks)

Photo by R. Diamante, Portland, Maine

My study of horticulture and living by the sea have given me a wealth of inspiration as well as a vocabulary of form, color, and texture that I rely on in my art making.

GAIL CROSMAN-MOORE
Vertebrae, 2003

Lampworked; silver fumed; borosilicate glass

6.4 x 1.9 cm

Photo by Charley Frieberg

BETH WILLIAMS
Heart Fibula, 2002

Lampworked; layered; surface decoration of fused 24k gold granules; etched; dichroic and soda-lime glass; gold-filled wire frame with pearl

5 x 5 x 1.3 cm

Photo by Paul Avis

My present work is a culmination of my background in lampworking and metalwork, as well as my fascination with form.

KATE FOWLE MELENEY
Petroglyph Goddess, 2002

Lampworked; enamel; ceramic overglazes; electroformed patinaed copper; soda-lime glass

7 x 2.9 cm

Photo by Jerry Anthony Photography

Once the pieces were electroformed, the beads were put back in the kiln and taken up high enough to burn the wax completely out from the inside of the electroformed handles, leaving the handles hollow. This creates an extremely light bead that's good for wearing but has the look of a heavily encrusted metal piece, like the old vessels you find at the bottom of the ocean, sort of a sculptural "trompe l'oeil," if you will.

ANN DAVIS
Shards From the Magellanic Clouds, 1992

Flameworked; frit; powders; handles and strips on companion beads formed from jeweler's wax and electroformed; soda-lime glass

5 x 2.5 x 1.3 cm (vessel); 3.2 x 1.3 cm (companion beads)

Photo by Jeff O'Dell

People laugh about "fondling" beads, but it's no joke! There is something very primal about holding and feeling the surface of a bead that goes back to our earliest existence on this planet. It's hard to look at a bead without touching it, so try to imagine the personal excitement you can get from actually creating them. It's fantastic!

INARA KNIGHT
Textures, 2002

Flameworked; tabular; frit and dichroic inclusions; surface trailing; surface decoration of copper electroformed patina; soda-lime glass

6.4 x 3.8 x .6 cm

Photo by Jeff O'Dell

I love to combine a variety
of techniques when
working with glass.
It allows me to create
unusual, stone-like pieces.

JEN ZITKOV
Day Dream, 2003

Lampworked; engraved;
soda-lime glass

2.2 x 2.2 x .9 cm

Photo by artist

W. BRAD PEARSON
Pulsar Series, 2003

Lampworked; acid etched;
soda-lime glass

1 x 5.5 cm

Photo by Taylor Dabney

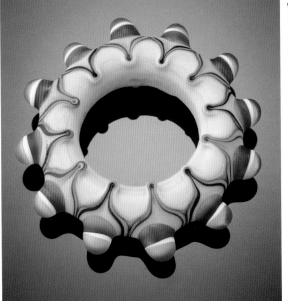

These vessels are an integration of various spiritual disciplines where prayers or blessings are placed in a container. Breath is our connection to all life.

LAURA LUBIN
Blessing Beads, 2001

Lampworked; latticino; dichroic and soda-lime glass; functional top with embedded stainless steel hardware

5 x 2.5 cm (each bead)

Photo by Susan Adams

59

For over 15 years I had been working in the "virtual" world of computer graphics. I was looking for an "actual" creative outlet when I took my first lampworking class. I've been happily melting glass since.

PAM HOGARTH
Kinetic Rings, 2002–03

Lampworked; raised dots; cylinders capped by disks; free-floating rings; soda-lime glass

1.9 x 1.6 x 1.9 cm (each bead)

Photo by artist

LESLI MASH
Asteroids, 2002

Lampworked; encased; dots;
soda-lime glass

Dimensions vary

Photo by Jerry Anthony Photography

These beads require good temperature control, not too hot or too cold. I use these in my jewelry but the colors make them fun just by themselves.

DONNA K. DREHER
Untitled, 1995

Lampworked; stringer; soda-lime glass

Dimensions vary

Photo by Mark Cheadle

A whimsical take on the glass bead
inspired by Islamic architecture.

PAT HOYT
Coral Angel, 2000

Lampworked; enamel; dichroic
and soda-lime glass

3.2 x 6.7 cm

Photo by Rich Images

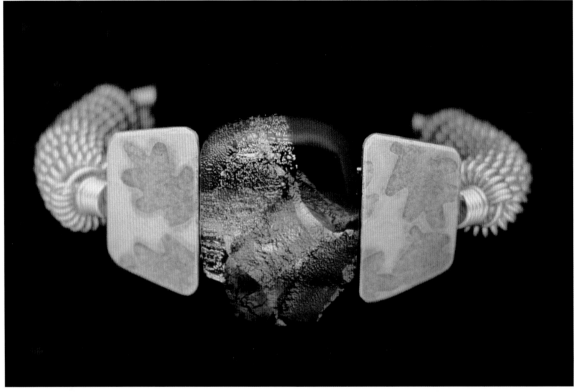

I love to work with glass, as it won't be dictated to, but requires you to work in cooperation with it.

CANDY BETH MICHALSKI
Patterned Metal Framed Bead Bracelet, 2003

Kiln-fused; carved and beveled; fire polished; soda-lime glass with dichroic coating; hand-fabricated bracelet with patterned sterling silver, handmade twisted beads, and pewter accent beads

17.8 cm (bracelet); 2.5 x 4.4 x .6 cm (focal bead)

Photo by artist

JANE PRAXEL
Monsoon, 2003

Lampworked; silver foil and stringer; dots; soda-lime glass

2.5 x 2 cm (largest bead)

Photo by David Orr

TRAVIS MEDAK
Indian Artifacts, 2003

Lampworked; cane; super-heated and stretched; tumbled; soda-lime glass

4.4 x 1.9 cm (largest bead)

Photo by artist

Beadmaking has become work and play, the process and final product a passion and an obsession.

ALETHIA DONATHAN
River Rock Series, 2003

Lampworked; enamel and mixed metal; soda-lime glass

6.4 x 1.3 cm

Photo by Azad

KATHLEEN DENNISON
Bubble Cuff Bracelet, 2002

Lampworked; hollow; goldstone dots; soda-lime glass; sterling silver and 14k gold

20.3 x 5 x 2.5 cm (bracelet); 2.5 x 1.8 cm (largest bead)

Photo by Ralph Gabriner

I've recently borrowed this philosophy: Don't sweat the petty things and don't pet the sweaty things.

SARA SALLY LaGRAND
Three Frogs, 2003

Lampworked; encased; hand-pulled stringer; enamel; soda-lime glass

2.5 x 2.5 cm

Photo by Rick McKibben

67

The threat of glass against skin creates an intriguing tension in this piece.

JENNIFER METTLEN NOLAN
Blue, 2003

Lampworked; layered; pulled dots; soda-lime glass; silver tubing and wire

10.2 x 22.9 x 27.9 cm

Photo by Rob Glover

ICHIRO IKEMIYAGI
Scroll, 2003

Lampworked; encased bead in
center; soda-lime glass

1.7 x 1.7 cm

Photo by artist

TANOUE EMIKO
Light, 2002–03

Lampworked; sandblasted; soda-lime glass

3 x 3 x 3 cm

Photo by Akiyama Hiroyuki

Nature—sky, space,
atmosphere, light, water, wind....

69

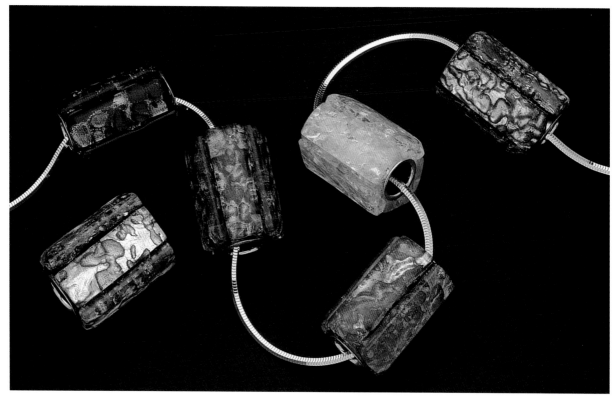

It's been said that my dichroic glass FireStones "combine luminous colors and otherworldly textures into a landscape of unexpected mystery." With the *Inlaid Beads,* I treat the glass slab as a semiprecious stone and use standard lapidary techniques to inlay the glass into the form of a bead.

NANCY GOODENOUGH
Inlaid Beads, 2000

Kilnformed; coldworked; inlaid; sterling silver core; FireStones (dichroic and soda-lime glass)

3.2 x 4.4 x 3.2 cm

Photo by George Post

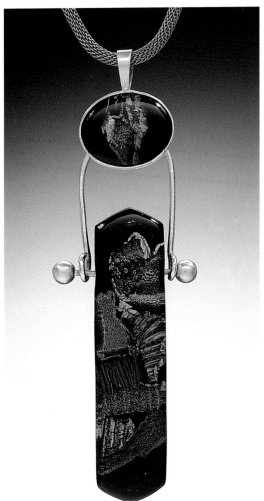

CANDY BETH MICHALSKI
Bezel Set Cab with Swinging Glass Bead Pendant, 2001

Kiln-fused; carved and beveled; fire polished; soda-lime glass with dichroic coating; hand-fabricated patterned sterling silver

8.9 x 1.9 x .6 cm

Photo by Ralph Gabriner

BETH BOAL
Copper Clouds and Copper Bubbles (Metallica Series), 2002

Lampworked; encased; copper and gold leaf; enamel; soda-lime glass

3.2 x 2.2 cm (left); 1.5 x 1 cm (right)

Photo by David Dale

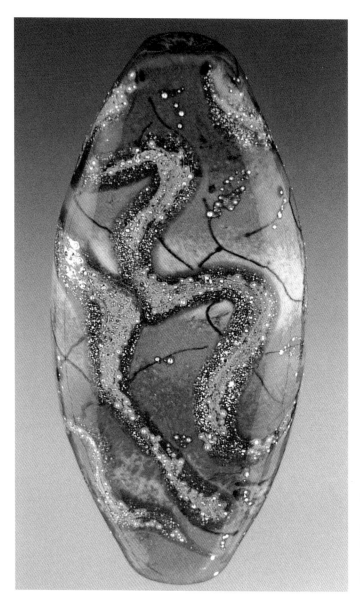

SANDRA SAYLOR SEAMAN
Water Abstract Tab, 2002

Lampworked; enamel powder; silver foil;
goldstone; soda-lime glass

4.5 x 2 x .7 cm

Photo by Jerry Anthony Photography

I wanted to draw a lively fish on a bead, without using millefiori, and made this one. The expression of each fish I draw is different.

SHIORI AICHI
Green Striped Fish, 2002

Flameworked; handmade stringer and ribbon cane; silver leaf; soda-lime glass

2.3 x 2.1 cm

Photo by artist

73

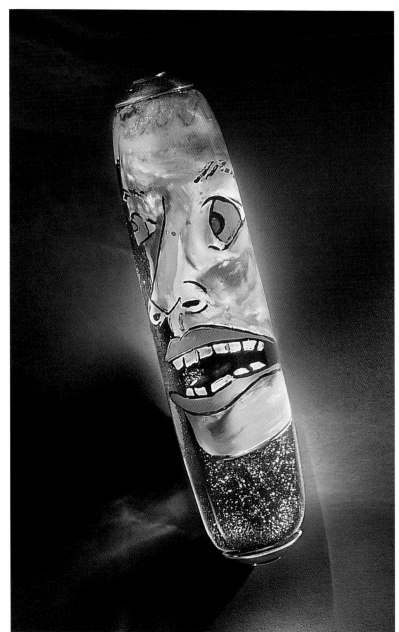

My inspiration for this work comes from my first visit to New York City in 1999. The people, the buildings…wow. My canvas is glass and my brush is the flame of a torch.

BRONWEN HEILMAN
Banshee, 2003

Flameworked; encased; layered enamel; dichroic and soda-lime glass; riveted sterling silver end caps

5 x 1.9 x 1.9 cm

Photo by Robin Stancliff

With these beads, my objective is to evoke the feeling and forms of fossils and seedpods found in nature.

MARJORIE BURR
Pods, 2003

Lampworked; dots; electroformed and patinaed copper; soda-lime glass

4.9 x 1.2 x 1.6 cm (largest bead)

Photo by Roger Schreiber

When the torchwork is done, you have a boring, striped cylinder. It's at the lapidary wheel that the fun begins, slicing through those canes you've made days earlier.

GREG GALARDY
Lapped Tubular Chevron, 2002

Lampworked; individually constructed and layered canes; coldworked; soda-lime glass

1.7 x 2.9 cm

Photo by artist

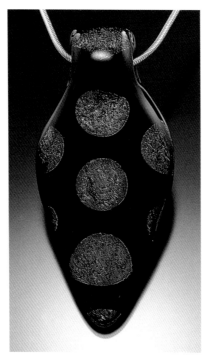

SUZANNE LEBERMAN
Dichro Dots Urn Pendant, 2003

Fused; dots; dichroic and fusible glass

7 x 3.2 cm

Photo by Larry Sanders

ELIZABETH B. CANNON
Dinosaur Eggs, 2003

Lampworked; encased; reduction frit;
soda-lime glass; crystal accents with
sterling silver spacers and toggle clasp

1.6 x 3 x 1.6 cm (focal bead);
1.5 x 1.5 x 1.5 cm (accent beads)

Photo by Jon Holloway

FUJIE KAWATA
Hana-No, 2003

Lampworked; millefiori; lead
and soda-lime glass

2.3 x 2 x 2 cm

Photo by artist

MICHELLE WALDREN
Ribbon Cane Bicone, 2003

Flameworked; encased; layered;
ribbon cane; soda-lime glass

3.2 x 3.2 cm

Photo by Roger Shrieber

AMY TRESCOTT
Water Garden, 2003

Lampworked; marbelized core;
soda-lime glass

1.3 x 1.5 x 1.5 cm

Photo by Doug Yaple

HEATHER TRIMLETT
Marble Beads, 2003

Lampworked; cane; soda-lime glass

1.25 x 1.25 cm (each bead)

Photo by Melinda Holden

I use glass to create specialty items for my jewelry to better convey the mood of a piece. The class clown is a loudmouth, cute and annoying at the same time, always the center of attention. The hat and eyes are lampworked beads. I combined glass with bright polymer clay to give the piece a youthful, playful appeal.

CHELSEA STONE
Class Clown, 2001

Lampworked; hollow; soda-lime glass; silver face from lost cast wax process; enamel, polymer clay, and plexiglass accents

7.6 x 5 x 5 cm

Photo by Robly Glover

MICHELLE WALDREN
Iris, 2003

Flameworked; layered; flower and stamen cane; palladium leaf; soda-lime glass

5.7 x 1.9 cm (left); 2.5 x 3.8 cm (right)

Photo by Roger Shrieber

TOMOKO TAKAHASHI
A Happy Whale, 2002

Torchworked; encased; mosaic cane; twistie; stringer; dots; goldstone powder; lead glass

1.9 x 1.9 x 1.9 cm

Photo by Masaaki Takahashi

WILLIAM C. STOKES III
Shell Game, 2002

Lampworked; sculpted; vacuum
formed; soda-lime glass

5 x 2.5 x 1.3 cm

Photo by artist

I love words and their derivations. With my husband, I invented the technique of making my own photos into a transfer image that can be fired onto enamel on my lamp-blown beads.

SHARI MAXSON HOPPER
Browsers Dictionary, 1998

Lamp blown; photographic transfer applied and fired; enamel; borosilicate glass

50.8 x 2.5 cm (necklace)

Photo by artist

Working in glass is like meditation.
I find myself lost in the molten
elements of flame and glass.

ROBERTA POFF
Ruby, 2003

Lampworked; sculpted; off-hand
technique; soda-lime glass

5 x 1.9 x 1.3 cm

Photo by Roger Schreiber

JUDIE MOUNTAIN
Glass Pendant, 2002

Lampworked; silver foil; dichroic
and soda-lime glass

5 x 3.8 x 1.3 cm

Photo by Tony Grant

I love dichroics! Usually they are
cased in clear glass to protect
the coating. This test result far
exceeds my expectations and I
plan to try more.

ALINE S. PETERSON
Naked Peacock Barrel, 2003

Lampworked; dichroic overlay with clear
dots; precious metals; soda-lime glass

2.5 x 2.5 x 2.5 cm

Photo by Dina Rossi

LISAJOY SACHS
Woof, 2002

Lampworked; sand etched; soda-lime glass; reversible pendant with sterling silver, 14k gold, azurite, malachite, and lapis lazuli

5.8 x 5.8 x 1.9 cm

Photo by Keith Meiser

NANCY SMITH
Untitled, 2003

Flameworked; stringer; soda-lime glass

4.2 x 2.5 x 2 cm

Photo by Steve Gyurina

AMY CASWELL
Hang in There, America Cat, 2003

Lampworked; sculpted; soda-lime glass

5 x 1.7 x 1.6 cm

Photo by Joseph Caswell

The bail is one of my "V-beads," lampworked using the Tobler triangle, a tool I designed in 1999.

WENDY TOBLER
Carousel Horse Pendant with V-Bead Bail, 2003

Lampworked; stringer; soda-lime glass

7 x 5 x 2.5 cm (focal bead);
2.5 x 4.4 x 1.3 cm (V-bead)

Photo by Reflections by Carey

CINDY BROWN
Cindybeads Assortment, 2002

Lampworked; twisted canes; dots; drawn
stringer; soda-lime glass

Dimensions vary

Photo by Azad

JAN HARRIS
Aboriginal Dreams, 2002

Lampworked; sculpted; raised
stringer; dots; raked; soda-lime glass

39.4 cm (necklace)

Photo by Laura Glaece

Each bead (more than 70) is made one at a time, no mold, then graduated from largest to smallest on cord. The snake's tongue clasps to its tail when worn. Nonpoisonous.

SAGE
Snake, 2003

Lampworked; etched; soda-lime glass

3.8 x 70 x 1.1 cm (necklace)

Photo by Tom Holland

DANIEL ADAMS
Offset Eye Beads, 2002

Lampworked; layered dots; soda-lime glass

5.7 x 1.9 x 1.9 cm (largest bead)

Photo by Roger Schreiber

EMIKO SAWAMOTO
Kabuki Dancer "Red Lion," 2002

Lampworked; sculpted; twisted cane; murrina;
gold foil; platinum leaf; soda-lime glass

6 x 3.8 cm

Photo by Rich Images

MICHAEL BARLEY
Jiordy, 2003

Lampworked; twisted dots; stringer; silver leaf; soda-lime glass

3.2 x 2.5 x 2.5 cm

Photo by Joan Beldin

ELIZABETH JOHNSON
Raspberry, Blackberry, and Blueberry Beads, 2003

Lampworked; hollow (raspberries and blackberries); solid (blueberries); acid-etched (raspberries); enameled (blueberries); soda-lime glass

Dimensions vary

Photo by Tomás del Amo

Unsuspecting people often scoop up these berry beads expecting a juicy snack. I love the humor and challenge of fooling the eye so completely that only a second (or third!) look reveals the truth.

NANCY PILGRIM
Cosmic Beads, 2002

Lampworked; hand-pulled star cane; soda-lime glass; sterling silver findings

50.8 cm (necklace);
2 cm (largest bead)

Photo by Jeff Scovil

95

DONNA NOVA
Holly Necklace, 2002

Lampworked; pressed leaves; dots;
soda-lime glass; sterling silver clasp

2.5 x 2.5 x 50.8 cm (necklace)

Photo by artist

TOM HOLLAND
Lapidaried Rondelle, 2002

Lampworked; murrini; coldworked;
soda-lime glass

5.2 x 5.2 x 1.1 cm

Photo by artist

MELINDA MELANSON
Garden Eye, 2003

Lampworked; sculpted; raked;
soda-lime glass

3.5 x 3 cm

Photo by Steve Gyurina

97

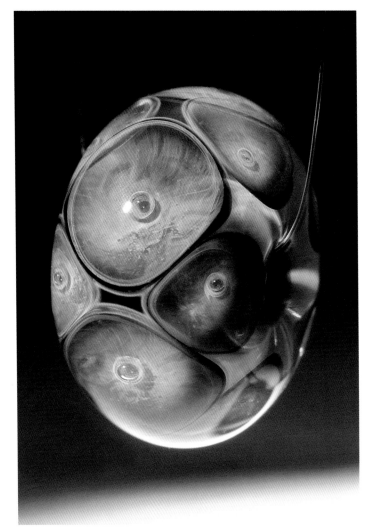

NORIKO ITO
Wind, 2003

Lampworked; lead glass

Photo by artist

Although I work in all different kinds of glass, the color variations and varying degrees of translucency that can be achieved with borosilicate glass make it my favorite.

SUE RICHERS ELGAR
Untitled, 2003

Flameworked; encased; plunged dots; borosilicate glass

2.5 x 1.3 x 2.5 cm

Photo by Steve Gyurina

After the first firing, when I can see
what the colors will really be like,
I get a feel for the theme of a set.
Backwards, maybe, but that's how
it happens.

JACKIE TITUS COOPER
The Bay, 2003

Kiln-fused; layered; cut; shaped;
coldworked; dichroic and fusible glass

5 x 3.8 x .9 cm (largest bead)

Photo by Don Faith

SYLVUS TARN
Triple Hollow Bead, 2003

Flameworked; triple hollow;
surface trailing; soda-lime glass

2.5 x 3.2 x 3.2 cm

Photo by artist

Love glass. Love metal. Why not fry glass onto metal? I'm known for the craters I create in kilnformed glass. These torch-fired beads replicate those strange textures in a totally different process. The breakthrough in the vitreous enamel layers was also a breakthrough for me: Now I'm an enamelist, too.

NANCY GOODENOUGH
Magister Ludi (Moonscape Bead Series), 2003

Torch-fired; pull-through technique; vitreous enamel on hollow copper bead; sterling silver spacers

2 x 3 x 2 cm (each bead)

Photo by Hap Sakwa

RYAN M. LAY
Double Cane Rings with Opal Center, 2003

Lampworked; encased; borosilicate glass; manmade opal

5 x 3.5 x 1.3 cm

Photo by artist

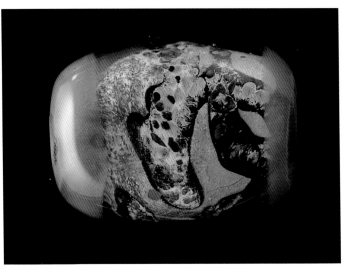

KIMBERLY ROGERS
Petrogyph, 2002

Lampworked; tabular; encased; enamel; frit; soda-lime glass

3 x 2.5 x 1.3 cm

Photo by Jack Dewitt

Making these spiral designs gave life to my beadmaking career. The unique design lends itself to many uses besides jewelry.

DONI HATZ
Collage of Montage Blown Beads,
1999–2003

Blown; cased; striped; twisted; sealed; shaped; dots; borosilicate glass tubing and color rods

Dimensions vary

Photo by Trevor Hart, Cincinnati, Ohio

103

JOHN OLSON
Oval Boro Bead, 2003

Blown; hollow; inside-out
technique; dots; gold and silver
fumed; borosilicate glass tubing

6.4 x 3.8 x 1.9 cm

Photo by Pati Walton

MARGO KNIGHT
Stained Glass Mosaic, 2002

Lampworked; fine silver foil;
soda-lime glass

4.1. x 1.3 x 1.3 cm

Photo by artist

I love playing with glass and silver.
The results can often seem alchemical.

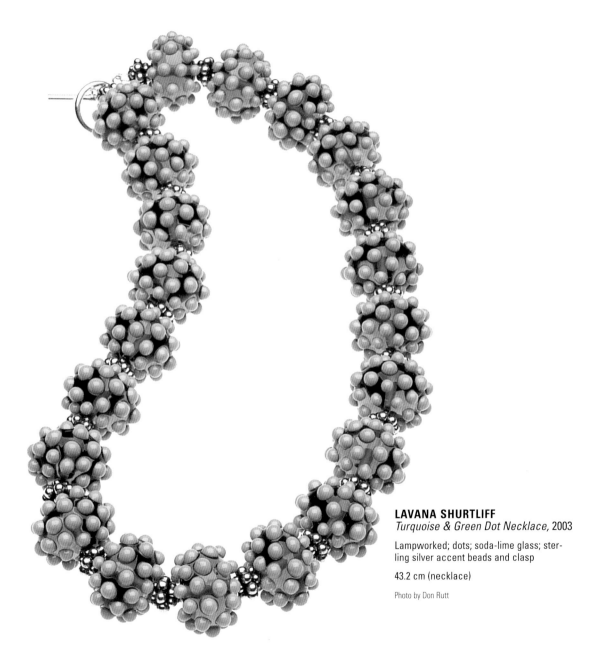

LAVANA SHURTLIFF
Turquoise & Green Dot Necklace, 2003

Lampworked; dots; soda-lime glass; sterling silver accent beads and clasp

43.2 cm (necklace)

Photo by Don Rutt

These beads were originally made for a juried jewelry show. They were so appealing that I've continued to make them, adding more colors.

BARBARA BECKER SIMON
California Bead Group, 2002–03

Lampworked; hollow; stringer; dots; twistie; enamel; soda-lime glass

Dimensions vary

Photo by Rob Stegmann

ALINE S. PETERSON
Curved Feather Fish in Blues & Greens, 2003

Lampworked; formed on curved mandrel; sculpted; ribbed canes; dots; stringer; goldstone; soda-lime glass

2.5 x 5 x 2.5 cm

Photo by Dina Rossi

107

I love working with hollow beads as the glass moves differently and the colors react differently from solid glass. This necklace is a reflection of the colors found in the oceans: coral, plants, and the waters themselves.

PAMELA DUGGER
Ocean Depths, 2001

Lampworked; hollow; layered powdered glass; soda-lime glass; sterling silver bead caps and clasp

45.6 cm (necklace); 3.2 cm (largest bead)

Photo by Jeffrey O'Dell

When I discovered flameworking, the term "playing with fire" gained new appreciation. My most satisfying results often come from those torch sessions that I approach with a playful attitude. In the best of those I become a partner with the glass and the flame—neither of us in total control—and magic results.

LARRY SCOTT
Bead, 1998

Flameworked; silver foil; soda-lime glass

3.2 x 2.1 x 1.3 cm

Photo by Roger Schreiber

MARGO KNIGHT
Planetary Landscape, 2003

Flameworked; fine silver foil; soda-lime glass

3.8 x 1.3 x 1.3 cm

Photo by artist

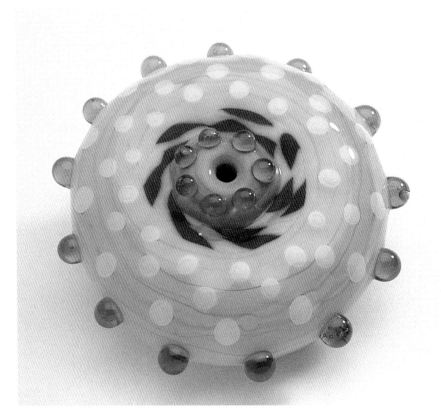

ELEANORE MACNISH
Swirl Series Hollow Bead, 2002

Lampworked; hollow; soda-lime glass

3 x 5.5 x 5.5 cm

Photo by David Nufer

HIROKO H. KOGURE
Untitled, 2003

Lampworked; twistie; dots; raked and
pulled; gold foil; etched; soda-lime glass

1.9 x 2.5 cm

Photo by artist

I believe displaying your beads is just as important as creating them. This bead tower is a pleasure piece; its sole purpose is to display my beads.

JENNIFER BROESKA
Bead Tower, 2002

Lampworked; encased; dots; soda-lime glass; handmade sterling silver accents

23.5 x 5 x 5 cm

Photo by Ken Mayer

CAROLANNE R. BOUCHLES
Patina Forest Bicone Series, 2003

Lampworked; frit; silver leaf; soda-lime glass

6.5 cm (each bead)

Photo by R. Diamante, Portland, Maine

I am always trying to unite metal with glass. The copper electroformed handles were inspired by Albert Paley's groundbreaking ironwork.

ANN DAVIS
Solar Eclipse, 1992

Flameworked; silver foil added and annealed; handles formed from jeweler's wax and electroformed; soda-lime glass

6.4 x 5 x 1.3 cm

Photo by Jeff O'Dell

113

MARYJANE MICHAUD
Evolution, 2003

Lampworked; twisted cane;
dots; borosilicate glass

3.8 x 2.5 x 2.5 cm

Photo by Steve Gyurina

GAIL CROSMAN-MOORE
Untitled, 2003

Lampworked; reduced; trailed;
borosilicate glass

7.6 x 1.9 cm

Photo by Charley Frieberg

I do a lot of watercolor painting; this method of bead construction allows me to "paint" my seascapes on each bead.

BILL IRVINE
Seascape Group, 2003

Lampworked; encased; silver foil; reduction powder; aventurine; soda-lime glass

Dimensions vary

Photo by Craig Wester

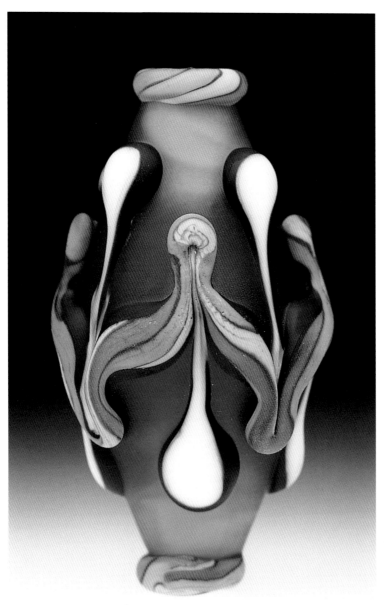

I came to lampworking from a background in digital graphic design and website development. It's incredibly satisfying to be able to hold my finished work in my hand and to know it won't be obsolete in a month.

ANDREA LAND
Southwest Arabesque, 2003

Lampworked; bicone; encased; raked stripes; handmade cane; dots; lightly etched; soda-lime glass

4.4 x 2.5 x 2.5 cm

Photo by Scott Smudsky

CAROLYN NOGA
African, 2003

Lampworked; sculpted;
soda-lime glass

2.5 cm

Photo by Painter Photography

117

LEIGH H. KEENAN
Star Series, 2000

Flameworked; layered;
marvered; borosilicate glass

2.5 x 2 cm

Photo by Cliff Pfeiffer

MICHAEL BARLEY
Henry, 2003

Lampworked; twisted dots; stringer;
silver leaf; soda-lime glass

4.4 x 4.4 x 1.3 cm

Photo by Joan Beldin

The prayer of fire, to melt to melt!

This is a poem by the late
potter Kanjiro Kawai. As a glass
worker, I must include a final line:
But not too much.

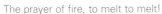

Inspired by the interaction between colors, form, and pattern, I love to create vibrant and unusual designs.

AMY JOHNSON
In Circles, 2003

Flameworked; paint detailed; soda-lime glass

43.2 x 4.4 x 3.8 cm (necklace)

Photo by Peter Tang

LISA KAN
Serenity Series, 2003

Flameworked; pulled and shaped;
custom-blended soda-lime glass;
silver spacers and findings

3.4 x 2.6 cm (largest bead)

Photo by Azad

NORIKO ITO
Flower in Water, 2003

Lampworked; lead glass

Photo by artist

I have always loved the play of light on transparent color, first as a watercolorist, and now as a glass beadmaker.

LOUAYNE RHODE
Seasons Hollows, 2002–03

Flameworked; hollow; surface decoration of dichroic strips, stringer, and dots; soda-lime glass; sterling silver wire and bead caps

2 x 2.5 x 1.5 cm

Photo by Don R. Young Photography

121

DAVID AND REBECCA JURGENS
Neptune's Gift, 2003

Flameworked; coil potting with off-mandrel
sculpture; borosilicate glass; sterling silver
and moonstone accents

6.4 x 3.8 x 3.8 cm

Photo by Rebecca Jurgens

SHELLY PAULETTE INSALL
Floral Fields, 2002

Lampworked; tabular; silver foil;
soda-lime glass

3.2 x 2.1 x .8 cm

Photo by artist

Accidents happen, but when a
tool stuck too long in the cooling
glass causes a "paisley tail" is it
really an accident, or the birth of
a new technique?

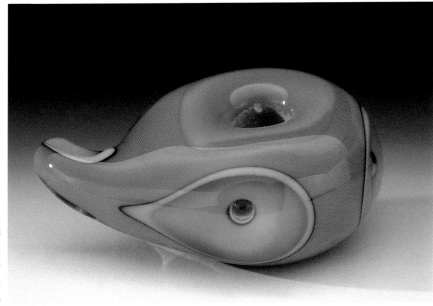

TAMRA TRAFFORD
The Paisley, 2003

Lampworked; bubble dots;
pulled; soda-lime glass

1.5 x 2.5 x 2 cm

Photo by Jerry Anthony Photography

LEA ZINKE
Spring Garden Beads, 2003

Lampworked; hollow; custom color
and cane; soda-lime glass

5 cm (vessel); 3.8 cm (largest bead)

Photo by Jerry Mesmer

WAYNE ROBBINS
Frog on a Leaf Bead, 2002

Lampworked; sculpted; fused;
frit; borosilicate glass

5 x 5 x 7 cm

Photo by Paul Avis

FUJIE KAWATA
Hana-Temari, 2003

Lampworked; millefiori; gold foil;
encased; lead and soda-lime glass

1.8 x 2 x 2 cm

Photo by artist

I wanted to push the definition of
a bead and create the ultimate
glass figure bead.

SERENA J.A. SMITH
Acrobat Beads, 2002

Lampworked; sculpted; soda-lime glass

7.6 x 3.8 x 2.5 cm (largest bead)

Photo by artist

NANCY SMITH
Ivory Rabbit, 2003

Flameworked; hollow;
soda-lime glass

2.4 x 3 x 1.8 cm

Photo by Steve Gyurina

WENDY TOBLER
Three Dogs, 2003

Lampworked; stringer;
soda-lime glass

5.7 x 8.2 x 1.9 cm
(largest bead)

Photo by artist

NANCY PILGRIM
Crowns, 2002

Lampworked; raked surface decoration; soda-lime glass

50.8 cm (necklace); 1.4 cm (beads)

Photo by Jeff Scovil

These are variations on my charm series. They are inspired by Venetian blown goblet stems.

MICHAEL "FIG" MANGIAFICO
Venetian, 2003

Torchworked; soda-lime glass

7.6 x 3.8 x .6 cm

Photo by Joelle Levitt

129

I like to start with a unique idea and figure out how to accomplish it technically. My four-hole beads are for beaders with imagination.

DIANE C. GILLESPIE
Four Hole Beads, 2001

Fused; four-hole beads with fiber-paper formed holes; dichroic and fusible glass

2.5 x 2.5 x 1.1 cm (each bead)

Photo by Jerry Downs

I love the light of the dichroic glass in random concert with the gold leaf.

CHRIS DARLING-DeLISLE
Midas Touch, 2003

Flameworked; dichroic glass inclusions; gold leaf; soda-lime glass

3.8 x 1.3 cm

Photo by R. Diamante, Portland, Maine

HARLAN SIMON
Three Beads, 2002

Lampworked; encased; soda-lime glass

1.9 x 1.9 x 1.3 cm (each bead)

Photo by Richard Reed, Rich Images

MARYBETH PICCIRELLI
Foil Filagree, 2003

Lampworked; stringer; silver leaf;
soda-lime glass

3.2 x 1.9 cm

Photo by Tim Thayer

EMILY MCKILLIP
Mythic Spaceball, 2003

Flameworked; hollow; reduction
frit; stringer; soda-lime glass

2.1 x 2.4 x 2.5 cm

Photo by Dan Lobdell

I am a glassblower (furnace worker). I make beads for the sheer fun of playing with glass on a smaller scale. I like to make jewelry and making my own beads as a centerpiece allows me a new design direction.

CONNIE CHRISTOPHER
Earth Form, 2003

Furnace worked; shaped; cut; dichroic and soda-lime glass; silver and pearl accents

Photo by Azad

133

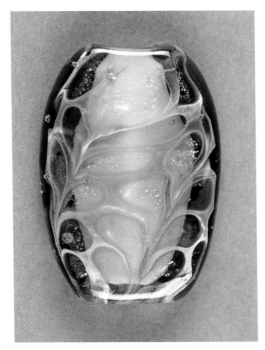

APRIL ZILBER
Untitled, 2001

Lampworked; silver foil;
soda-lime glass

3.8 x 1.9 x .6 cm

Photo by artist

TOM HOLLAND
Bent Family Cane on Foil, 2003

Lampworked; murrini; foil;
coldworked; soda-lime glass

2.8 x 5.8 x 1.2 cm

Photo by artist

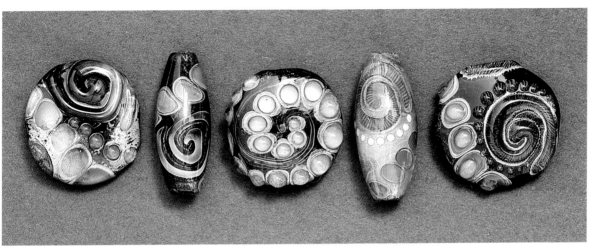

ANDREA GUARINO-SLEMMONS
Nautilus Collage, 2003

Lampworked; silvered stringer; gold
and silver fumed; soda-lime glass

Dimensions vary

Photo by artist

Our first thought is that glass is
transparent. It is, of course, also
opaque. This window bead plays off our
expectations of what glass should be.

LARRY SCOTT
Window Bead, 2002

Flameworked; silver foil; soda-lime glass

5.2 x 1.2 x 1.2 cm

Photo by Roger Schreiber

135

DOLLY AHLES
Enchanted Garden, 2003

Lampworked; encased; stringer;
dichroic and soda-lime glass

3.8 x 3.8 cm

Photo by Jeff Scovil

KIM FIELDS
*Peach Floral with
Blueberries,* 2002

Lampworked; etched;
striped canes; encased
stringers; soda-lime glass

3.6 x 1.2 x 1.2 cm

Photo by Tom Van Eynde

My work is about transformation.
I love to transform rods of
glass into fluid, organic forms,
combining realistic detail and
whimsical designs.

BECKY SCHUPBACH
Tree Goddesses, 2003

Flameworked; layered; surface
decoration from stringers, raking,
and sculpting; soda-lime glass

3.8 x 3.5 x 2.2 cm (vessel);
3.5 x 3.2 x .9 cm (bead)

Photo by Geoffrey Carr

These montage spirals are awesome to create, giving so much life to the glass.

DONI HATZ
Hand Blown Montage Beads,
1999–2003

Blown; cased; striped; twisted;
sealed; shaped; dots; borosilicate
glass tubing

Dimensions vary

Photo by Trevor Hart, Cincinnati, Ohio

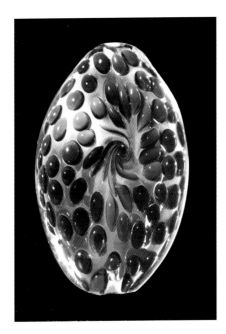

JOHN OLSON
Bullit Train, 2003

Blown; hollow; inside-out technique; gold and silver fumed; borosilicate glass tubing

5.7 x 3.2 x 1.9 cm

Photo by Tomās Del Amo

The interplay of color and light in glass is the driving inspiration for my work—just as color and light interplay in nature and my gardens, always creating new perspectives on established ideas and views.

BETH WILLIAMS
Vessel Bead, 2003

Lampworked; layered; plunged dots; surface decoration of applied silver and fused gold granules; dichroic and soda-lime glass

3.8 x 3.2 x 1 cm

Photo by Steve Gyurina

EMIKO NUMATA
Ancient Arizona, 2001

Lampworked; handmade millefiori;
lead glass

2.6 x 2.3 x 1.5 cm

Photo by MGM (JAPAN)

ELEANORE MACNISH
Complex Flower Beads, 2002

Lampworked; plunged; soda-lime glass

1.5 x 4 x 4 cm

Photo by David Nufer

ANDREA GUARINO-SLEMMONS
Multi-Dot Bead, 2003

Lampworked; dots; soda-lime glass

5.4 x 2.5 cm

Photo by Whit Slemmons

KAREN J. LEONARDO
Sea Squid Series, 2003

Lampworked; layered; reduction
frit; silver foil; palladium leaf;
dichroic glass

3.2 x 1.8 cm

Photo by artist

I love working with borosilicate glass because of the wonderfully organic tones it produces, and because each borosilicate bead is always unique.

AMY HAFTKOWYCZ
Assorted Borosilicate Beads, 2003

Lampworked; layered; borosilicate glass

Dimensions vary

Photo by Steven Waskow

143

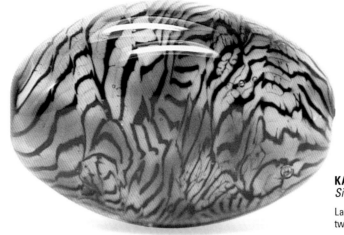

KATHY PERRAS
Siberian Tiger Print Bead, 2002

Lampworked; encased; color
twists; soda-lime glass

3.8 x 2.6 x 1.5 cm

Photo by Shaun Jarvis

VER ET FRAMBOISE
Disc, 2002

Lampworked; silver; soda-lime glass

4 cm

Photo by artist

MARCIA J. PARKER
*Amber and Black Detailed Dot
Beads,* 2003

Lampworked; layered, raised,
plunged, and twisted dots; aventurine;
soda-lime glass

2.9 x 1.9 x 2.9 cm (left);
2.5 x 1.7 x 2.5 cm (right)

Photo by Kallan Nishimoto

My beads are colored solely with metals. I love the magic that happens when hot glass is mixed with metal, and the challenge of using chemistry as a design element.

RENÉ ROBERTS
Beads from the Stonework Series,
1997–2001

Flameworked; stringer; metal leaf and oxides (copper, fine silver, iron, and 24k gold); soda-lime glass

5.7 cm (largest bead)

Photo by Hap Sakwa

AMY LEMAIRE
Calligraphy Beads, 2003

Flameworked; silver core;
soda-lime glass

1 x 1 x 1 cm

Photo by artist

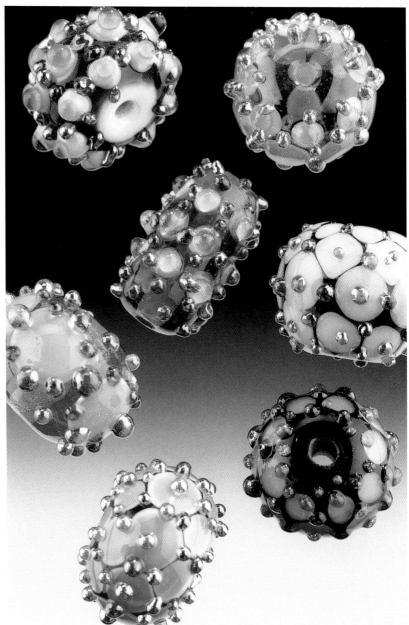

My beadmaking motto is:
The shinier, the better.

KAREN WOJCINSKI
Jewels, 2003

Lampworked; encased dots; reduction
frit stringer; soda-lime glass

1.5 x 1 x 1 cm

Photo by Jerry Anthony Photography

MONA LINDSEY GOLLAN
Talisman II, 2003

Lampworked; encased; stringer; hand-pulled cane; silver foil; soda-lime glass

4.2 x 1.3 cm

Photo by artist

PATRICIA ZABRESKI VENALECK
Baby Blue Floral, 2003

Lampworked; layered; stringer; dots; soda-lime glass; crystal and silver spacers, silver clasp

17.8 cm (bracelet); 1.3 x 2 cm (focal bead)

Photo by Patrick Buschmohle

KRISTINA LOGAN
Three Ivory Totem Beads, 2003

Lampworked; soda-lime glass

7.3 x 1.9 x 1.9 cm (each bead)

Photo by Paul Avis

CONSTANCE PAULDING
Hematite Dots on Ivory, 2002

Flameworked; hollow; reduced dots; soda-lime glass;
handmade clasp, sterling silver accents

48.3 cm (necklace)

Photo by Jeff Baird

These mosaic glass canes were made
by creating design bundles from flat
glass and pulling them into cane, using
a glory hole.

JAMES ALLEN JONES
Mosaic Glass Cane, 2002

Kilnformed; heated in glory hole;
hand-pulled cane; fusible glass

1 to 4 cm (diameter)

Photo by artist

CAROLYN NOGA
Cry, 2003

Lampworked; sculpted; latticino; soda-lime glass

3.8 cm

Photo by Painter Photography

JULIE CLINTON
Frogworld, 1997

Lampworked; sculpted; off-hand technique; glass and luster powder; cane; soda-lime glass

3.8 x 3.8 cm

Photo by artist

The inspiration for this bead came from growing my bonsai plants.

LEAH FAIRBANKS
Cotton Aster Bonsai, 2001

Lampworked; glass powders; gold foil; dichroic and soda-lime glass

7.6 cm

Photo by George Post

TOSHIKI UCHIDA
Ancient Flower, 2002

Lampworked; handmade millefiori; soda-lime glass

2.3 x 2.3 x 2.3 cm

Photo by artist

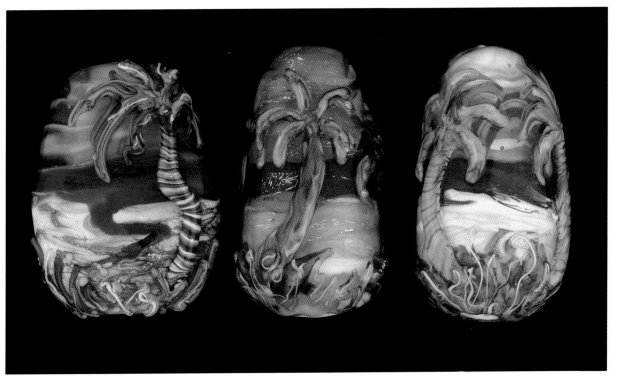

TERRE BEASLEY
Seascape, 2002

Lampworked; custom color stringer;
hand-pulled cane; silver leaf; dichroic
and soda-lime glass

3.8 x 2.2 x 2.2 cm

Photo by PM Artwork

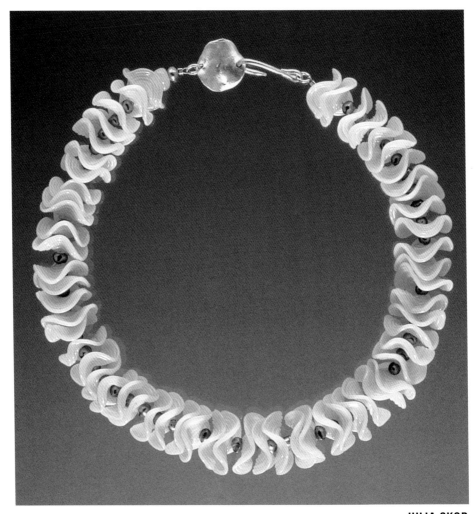

JULIA SKOP
Potato Chips: Sea Foam, 2002

Flameworked; soda-lime glass; metal
clay clasp and blue pearls

45.7 cm (necklace); 3.1 cm (largest bead)

Photo by Chris Bretschneider

No matter how much planning and forethought I put into these beads, the final product is always somewhat of a surprise.

GREG GALARDY
Tubular Eggs, 2002

Lampworked; individually constructed canes; layered; coldworked; soda-lime glass

Dimensions vary

Photo by Doc Damage

This one came from a drawing done back in my drawing days, based on eyes from three spirits peering through from another place.

SAGE
Trinity, 2003

Lampworked; dots; soda-lime glass

2.8 x 3.2 x .8 cm

Photo by Tom Holland

NANCY DRIVER
Moonlight Water, 2003

Lampworked; encased; stringer; silver leaf; soda-lime glass

3 x 2 cm

Photo by Roger Davis

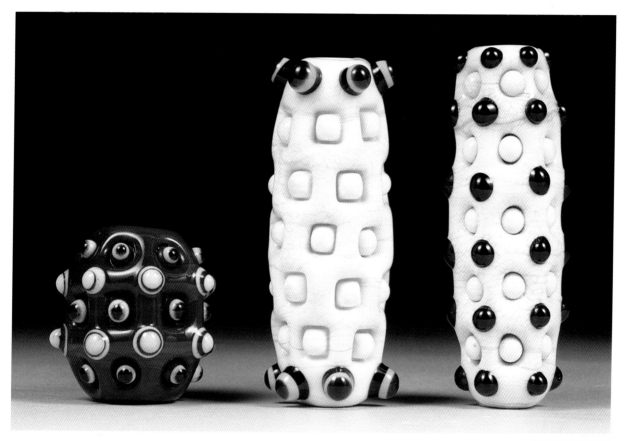

LYNNE ELLIOTT
Primitive Series, 2002

Lampworked; imprinted with surface dots; soda-lime glass

4.4 x 1.9 x 1.9 cm (largest bead)

Photo by David Orr

In my work I always try to combine glass with silver or gold—to make my work distinctive—and I don't mind a bit of humor.

LISE AAGAARD
Chicken Ring, 2000

Lampworked; sculpted; sterling silver (lost wax technique)

Photo by Dirk Burkman

My work in glass reflects my love of color and my belief that art should be fun.

FAITH WICKEY
Heart, 2000

Lampworked; stringer; twistie; soda-lime glass

3.2 x 3.2 x .6 cm

Photo by Jerry Anthony Photography

RENÉE HOLOUBEK
Tangled Jewels, 2003

Lampworked; tabular; silver foil;
reduction frit; soda-lime glass

4.1 x 1.3 x 1.9 cm

Photo by Mike Bowden

Flamework has become a type
of meditation for me; you must
be in the present and mindful
throughout the process.

LANI CHING
Silver Fumed MC Bicone, 2001

Flameworked; fumed; silver foil;
twists; soda-lime glass

3.8 x 1.6 cm

Photo by Teresa Sullivan

All of my broken beads are tossed into my garden. I'm creating a future archeological site —"Ancient North American Glass Beadmaker of the 21st Century A.D."

JANICE PEACOCK
Ancient Mask Series, 2003

Lampworked; sculpted; reduction powder; soda-lime glass

6.4 x 2.5 x 1.9 cm (each bead)

Photo by artist

163

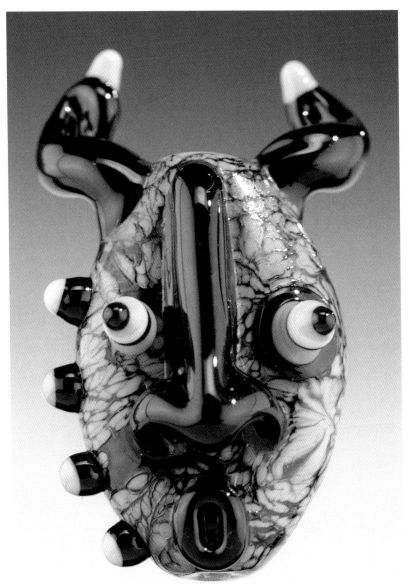

MARY H. KARG
Mask Bead, 2002

Lampworked; stringer; soda-lime glass

3.8 x 2.5 cm

Photo by Jerry Anthony Photography

KATHERINE ABBOTT
Untitled, 2002

Lampworked; dots; silver foil; soda-lime glass

3.2 x 1.5 cm

Photo by Dina Rossi

JARED BRODY
Peacock, 2003

Blown; reversed axis fish scale;
color fade; borosilicate glass

5 x 6.5 x 1.5 cm

Photo by Jen Zitkov

165

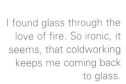

I found glass through the love of fire. So ironic, it seems, that coldworking keeps me coming back to glass.

BEAU
Tryfaceted, 2000

Lampworked; murrini; ground facets; soda-lime glass

2.5 x .5 x 2.5 cm

Photo by Tom Holland

AKIKO ISONO
Frog is Holding Sea Shore, 2003

Lampworked; sculpted; silver foil; soda-lime glass

3 x 3 x 3 cm

Photo by artist

KAREN OVINGTON
Untitled, 2002

Lampworked; enamel; frit;
soda-lime glass

63 cm (necklace)

Photo by Robert K. Liu

These beads scream fun and funky. This whimsical style is what attracted me to lampworking several years ago, and I still love it.

AMY TRESCOTT
Edible, 2003

Lampworked; soda-lime glass; crystal, vintage bead, and seed bead accents

17.8 cm (bracelet); 8 x 11 x 11 mm (beads)

Photo by Doug Yaple

My work is about color and form. I have always approached each bead as a separate tiny, self-contained sculpture.

W. BRAD PEARSON
Glyph Series Bead, 2003

Lampworked; overlapping dots; acid etched; soda-lime glass

2.9 x 1.9 cm

Photo by Taylor Dabney

SABRINA PIERSON
Love Circle, 2003

Lampworked; dots; stringer; frit; metal oxides;
soda-lime glass

2.3 x 1 x .4 cm (largest bead)

Photo by Kate Baldwin

These are mushrooms, fungi, worms, seeds, sprouts, and roots. It expresses the ecosystem under the fallen leaves.

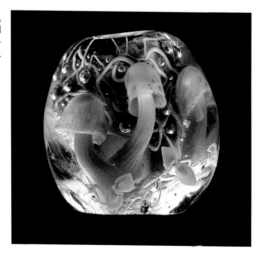

CINDY SAILOR
iLucidareî, 2002

Lampworked; dichroic and soda-lime glass; hand-patterned sterling silver disks and wire

3.8 x 1.5 x 1.5 cm

Photo by Azad

AKIKO ISONO
Cycle—Under the Fallen Leaves, 2003

Lampworked; sculpted; encased; soda-lime glass

2.5 x 2.5 x 2.5 cm

Photo by Masato Ogawa and Shoji Hori

ELOISE COTTON
Abstract Bead Necklace, 2001

Lampworked; stringer; frit; shards; encased;
borosilicate glass; steel cable

61 cm (necklace); 1.3 x 1.9 cm (each bead)

Photo by Hap Sakwa

While working in the flame it's hard to see what the enamels will look like when reacting to the transparent glass. It's always a surprise the next day, taking the beads out of the annealing oven to reveal a true galaxy of colors. No two are ever the same.

TERESA BRITTAIN
Tabular Web Bead with Borders, 2003

Lampworked; dots; stippled web effect; silver leaf; soda-lime glass

4.2 x 2.1 x .9 cm

Photo by Robert Batey

HEATHER J. RANDALL
Topaz Galaxy, 2002

Lampworked; encased; enamel powder; gold leaf; dichroic stringer; soda-lime glass

4 x 1.9 cm

Photo by Allen Bryan

I love both the process and the effect
of matting and faceting these florals.
Spending up to two hours at the torch
creating the layers and depth, only to
envelop them with a final coat of color,
is always a leap of faith! But the hours
then spent "unwrapping the package" at
the lapidary wheel make it all worthwhile.

KIM WERTZ
Window Floral, 2003

Lampworked; layered; coldworked;
soda-lime glass

3.6 x 2.4 cm

Photo by Greg Galardy

173

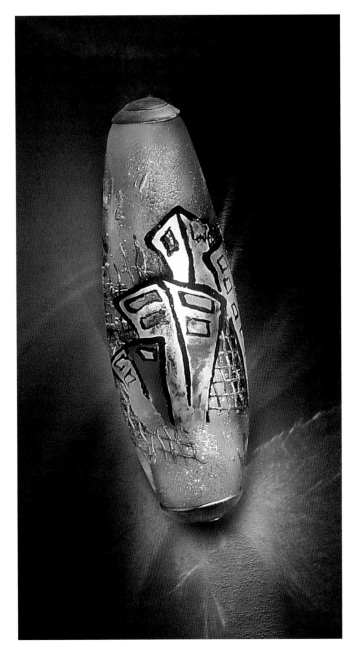

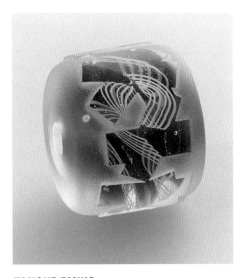

TANOUE EMIKO
Space, 2002–03

Lampworked; sandblasted; soda-lime glass

3 x 3 x 3 cm

Photo by Akiyama Hiroyuki

BRONWEN HEILMAN
Escape From the Gated Community, 2002

Flameworked; encased; enamels; copper mesh; dichroic and soda-lime glass; riveted sterling silver end caps

5 x 1.9 x 1.9 cm

Photo by Robin Stancliff

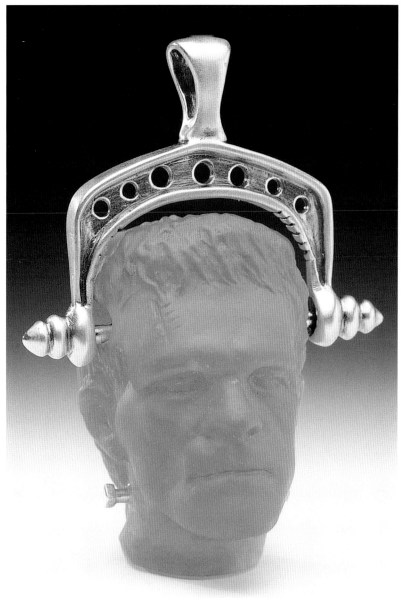

I've always identified with Frankenstein, scary on the outside but good on the inside, very misunderstood. Not to mention that we have also both been chased by angry villagers with pitchforks!

GREGG BURGARD
Frankenstein, 2002

Cast; pâte de verre technique; lead glass; sterling silver bail and neck bolts

5.7 x 3.8 x 3.2 cm

Photo by Jerry Anthony Photography

MARCIA KMACK
Beads from Marcia's Class
"Lots of Dots," 2003

Flameworked; stringer; dots; raked
and plunged; soda-lime glass

Dimensions vary

Photo by Buddy Hewitt

NANCY PILGRIM
Fantasy Flowers, 2002

Lampworked; hand-pulled face cane; soda-lime glass

50.8 cm (necklace); 1.4 cm (beads)

Photo by Jeff Scovil

Our beadmaking stems from a strong interest in bead trade and history, and a fascination with Italian glass technique and tradition. Making beads is a natural extension of our other blown work in which we also make use of complex glass cane. Our artistic goal is to create beads that evoke wonder and incredulity from complexity, detail, and exquisite color combinations.

MARY MULLANEY AND RALPH MOSSMAN
Chevron Beads, 1998

Blown; drawn; coldworked; tumble polished; soda-lime furnace glass

Dimensions vary

Photo by Robert K. Liu

I turned 40 in 2002, and decided to make a piece celebrating the fact that I was beginning my midlife party!

KELLY SCHROEDER
Midlife Party!, 2002

Lampworked; surface decoration includes metal inclusions, foil, stringer, and dots; soda-lime glass; handbuilt copper wire frame with various bead accents

76.2 x 25.4 cm

Photo by Azad

179

My desire is to create fun and funky objects using both my beadmaking and my metalsmithing skills. Playing with fire is mesmerizing and I am amazed that I can manipulate it to create things of beauty.

MISTY SHWIYYAT
Simple Adornment, 2003

Torchworked; stringer; dots and raised dots; etched; soda-lime glass; handmade sterling silver bracelet with rivets

Dimensions vary

Photo by Summer Harris

CATHARINE WEAVER
The Gilded Cage, 2003

Flameworked; hollow-core construction; lattice work; borosilicate glass

2.5 x 2.9 cm

Photo by Harold Wood

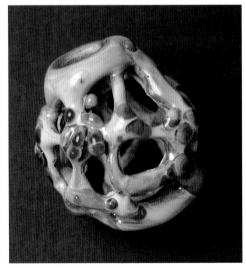

When I was trying to figure out how to make insects in glass, my beads started to grow tentacles and wings.

MICHAEL "FIG" MANGIAFICO
Dodecapod, 2003

Torchworked; acid washed; soda-lime glass

8.9 x 7.6 x 8.9 cm

Photo by Joelle Levitt

181

This is part of a series of 18 standing ring sculptures. When crowded together they create a quirky collection.

KATHRYN WARDILL
Tall Bead Ring Series, 2001

Flameworked; hollow and solid beads; sculpted; stringer; soda-lime glass; sterling silver and silverplated bronze

12 x 4 x 3 cm (each ring)

Photo by artist

I made this bead for the International Society of Glass Beadmakers' "Obsession" exhibit, and was going for maximum 3-D effect, so I had to learn how to work using components. If you break a complicated design into component parts you'll get precision and extra detail, but the panic and chaos of putting it all together! I almost didn't survive the experience....

SHARON PETERS
In the Shallows, needeep, needeep, 2002

Lampworked; sculpted; separate components added to encased base; soda-lime glass

3.8 x 3.8 x 4.4 cm

Photo by Janice Peacock

JANE PRAXEL
Borosilicate Medley, 2003

Lampworked; encased; raised and
poked dots; frit; borosilicate glass

1.9 x 2.8 cm (largest bead)

Photo by David Orr

I love oak trees, and their acorns come in various shapes, sizes, and colors. They're the perfect inspiration for a bead.

JOYCE ROOKS
Acorn Beads, 2002

Lampworked; enamel; soda-lime glass

Dimensions vary

Photo by artist

185

BILL IRVINE
Sea Urchin Group, 2003

Lampworked; sculpted; silver foil;
reduction stringers; soda-lime glass

3.2 x 1.9 cm (each bead)

Photo by Craig Wester

A recent workshop in sand-blasting beads compelled me to try new things, including this design in honor of the fishermen in my life.

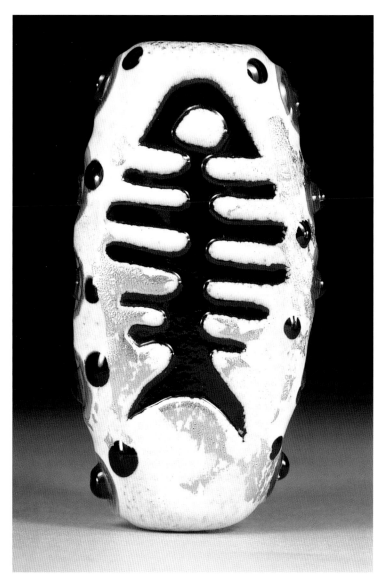

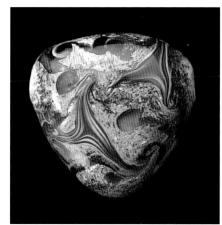

LISA SCHREMP MOSSER
Stone Nebula Bead, 2002

Lampworked; stringer; silver leaf; enamel; soda-lime glass

2 x 2.1 x 1.3 cm

Photo by Richard Nelson

LYNNE ELLIOTT
Fishbone, 2003

Lampworked; enameled; gold leaf; sand-blasted; fire polished; soda-lime glass

2.5 x 4.4 x 1.3 cm

Photo by David Orr

Having worked as a furnace glassblower, I enjoy working on sculptural pieces.

LISA ST. MARTIN
Amethyst Perfume Vial, 2002

Lampworked; encased; shaped and snipped; dichroic glass inclusions; soda-lime glass

7.6 x 3.8 x 1.9 cm

Photo by Jerry Anthony Photography

My beads are often mistaken for semiprecious stones. I play upon that illusion in my *Mythical Stones* series.

TOSHIKI UCHIDA
Sea Jelly, 2002

Lampworked; hand-pulled cane;
soda-lime glass

2.1 x 2.1 x 2.1 cm

Photo by artist

KARAN DOTSON
Blue and Green Mythical Stone, 2003

Flameworked; built off the end of the mandrel;
tapered; enamel; soda-lime glass; pewter beads
and bead cap, silver wire, and waxed linen cord

6.4 x 1.3 x 1.3 cm

Photo by Robert Batey

I created the clam beads for an exhibit at the George Ohr Museum in Biloxi, Mississippi. Humor—don't leave home without it!

ANGI GRAHAM
Tex the Texas Clam, 2000

Flameworked; borosilicate glass; stone pendant with twisted sterling silver wire and antique buttons

7 cm

Photo by artist

SHERYLL HUBBARD
Which, 2003

Lampworked; sculpted; multiple stringers; soda-lime glass

3.2 x 2.5 x 1.9 cm

Photo by Deanna Rossi

OFILIA J. CINTA
Hollow Lampwork Fish Bead, 2002

Lampworked; hollow; murrini; soda-lime glass

4.4 x 4.7 x 1.6 cm

Photo by Rich Images

JOHN WINTER
Lithos, 2003

Lampworked; metal foils oxidized on surface;
chemically etched; soda-lime glass

1.9 x 1.3 cm (each bead)

Photo by Tommy Olof Elder

STEVI BELLE-DAVIDSON
Ancient Bottle, 2002

Flameworked; blown; metal leaf and powders; copper electroplated with applied patina; soda-lime glass

8.9 x 3.2 x 2.5 cm

Photo by Jerry Anthony Photography

Hollow beads are great for creating size without too much weight. I like using transparent glass under the powder so there's still some light coming through the bead.

TERESA BRITTAIN
Hollow Bead with Glass Powders and Gold Leaf, 2003

Lampworked; hollow; surface decoration of 22k-gold leaf, glass powder, and stringer; soda-lime glass

1.9 x 3 cm

Photo by Robert Batey

MARY H. KARG
Bali Dreams, 2002

Lampworked; stringer; silver leaf; soda-lime
glass; silver and citrine accents

45.7 x 5 x 2.5 cm (necklace)

Photo by Jerry Anthony Photography

SHERRY PLOOF
Name Beads, 2002

Lampworked; silvered stringer;
soda-lime glass

Dimensions vary

Photo by R. Diamante, Portland, Maine

195

AMY JOHNSON
Counting, 2003

Flameworked; dots; soda-lime glass

41.9 x 2.5 x 3.2 cm (necklace)

Photo by Peter Tang

Having a background in fiber arts, I combine the elements of texture and color in my beads.

LISA NIVEN KELLY
Pisces, 2003

Lampworked; silver foil; fine silver wire; dichroic and soda-lime glass

3 x 1 x 2.5 cm

Photo by artist

LAURI COPELAND
Silkstone, n.d.

Lampworked; layered; etched; faceted windows; patterned dichroic core; soda-lime glass

6.5 x 1.8 x 1.8 cm

Photo by artist

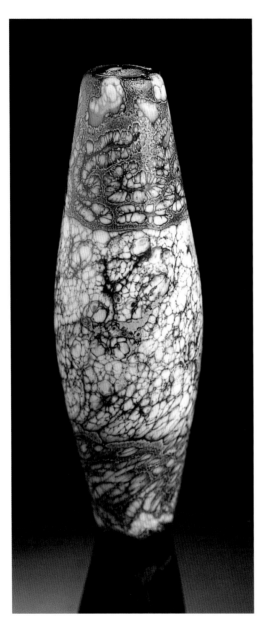

TERESA BRITTAIN
Bead with Borders and Enamels, 2003

Lampworked; silvered ivory and enamel stringer stippling; silver leaf; enamel; soda-lime glass

3.7 x 1.2 cm

Photo by Robert Batey

KARAN DOTSON
Grey and Pink Shell, 2003

Flameworked; built off the end of the mandrel; twistie; acid-dipped finish; soda-lime glass; silver wire, pewter spacers, and glass and seed bead accents

4.4 x 2.5 x 2.2 cm

Photo by Robert Batey

ROXANNE TAYLOR
Ambersheen, 2003

Lampworked; silver leaf; soda-lime glass

5 x 1.2 x 1.2 cm (largest bead)

Photo by John Bonath

HEATHER J. RANDALL
Copper Canyon, 2003

Flameworked; encased; enamel powder; gold foil;
dichroic stringer; soda-lime glass; strung with
seed beads and crystals

45.7 cm (necklace); 3.8 x 2.5 x 1.3 cm (bead)

Photo by Allen Bryan

This piece is an explosion of bubbles and seaweed.

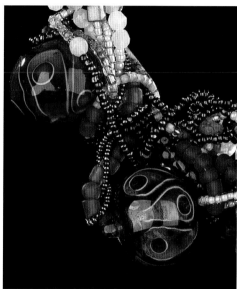

TAMARA MELCHER
Queen of the Deep, 2003

Torchworked; hollow; stringer; powder; soda-lime glass; seed and semiprecious bead accents with sterling silver clasp

24.1 x 14 x 2.5 cm (necklace)

Photo by David Egan Photography

KAREN WOLFFIS
Enya, 2003

Lampworked; layered; raised dots;
stringer; silver foil; soda-lime glass

20.3 cm (bracelet)

Photo by artist

DAVID JOHNSON
Lampworked Beads, 2003

Lampworked; dot techniques;
soda-lime glass

1.5 x 2.5 cm (largest bead)

Photo by Debbie Austin

REIJIRO WADA
Flower in Stillness Wood, 2003

Lampworked; encased; twisted stringer;
handmade millefiori; soda-lime glass

2.5 x 2.6 cm (largest bead)

Photo by Tatsuya Higuchi (246 Studio)

CYNTHIA LIEBLER SAARI
Treasure, 2003

Lampworked; surface reduction; encased
copper mesh; soda-lime glass

5.7 x 1.9 x 1.9 cm

Photo by Ralph Gabriner

TOSHIKI UCHIDA
Ancient Flower, 2002

Lampworked; handmade millefiori; soda-lime glass

2.2 x 2.2 x 2.2 cm

Photo by artist

BARBARA A. WRIGHT
Lampworked Glass Bead Necklace, 1999

Lampworked; soda-lime glass; amethyst, metal
beads, and handmade sterling silver chain

55 cm (necklace)

Photo by Hap Sakwa

This molten material is a terrific vehicle for expressing my notion of birth, rebirth, and emergence through allusion to primitive life forms.

GAIL CROSMAN-MOORE
Dagger Boa, 2003

Lampworked; borosilicate glass

Crochet by Karen Flowers

61 cm (neckpiece)

Photo by Charley Frieberg

207

SYLVUS TARN
Triple Hollow Beads, 2003

Flameworked; triple hollow;
surface trailing; soda-lime glass

2.5 x 3.2 x 3.2 cm (each bead)

Photo by artist

SHIORI AICHI
Peach Fish, 2002

Flameworked; handmade stringer and ribbon cane; baking soda; soda-lime glass

2 x 2.3 cm

Photo by artist

RYAN M. LAY
Switchback Spiral with Dichroic Background, 2003

Lampworked; spiral trails; dichroic glass, borosilicate glass tubing and color rods

5 x 3.5 x 1.6 cm

Photo by artist

209

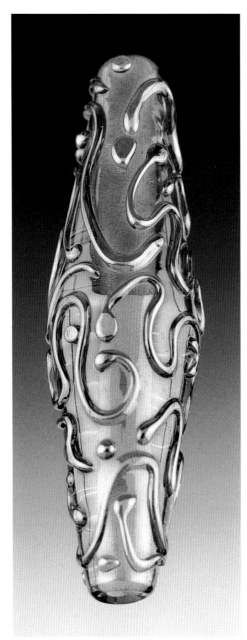

I love the sleek shape of the bicone.
Gold fuming shifts the color—
always interesting.

KAYE HUSKO
Tuscany Garden, 2003

Lampworked; tabular; encased;
silver foil; soda-lime glass

2.2 x 2 x .9 cm

Photo by artist

LISA ST. MARTIN
Labradorite Lace, 2001

Lampworked; bicone; surface stringer decoration;
24k-gold fumed; soda-lime glass

6.4 x 1.9 x 1.9 cm

Photo by Jerry Anthony Photography

MONIQUE Da SILVA
Starlite Gardens, 2003

Lampworked; encased; plunged;
cane; palladium leaf; cubic zirconia;
soda-lime glass

6.5 x 2 x 2 cm

Photo by artist

YOSHIKO SHIIBA
CHIGUSA, n.d.

Lampworked; murrini;
soda-lime glass

1.2 x 1.2 x 4.5 cm

Photography unattributed

DEBORAH N. KATON
*Contemporary Glass Artifacts
Series II,* 2002

Lampworked; enamels; baking
soda; soda-lime glass

6.4 cm

Photo by Peg Fetter

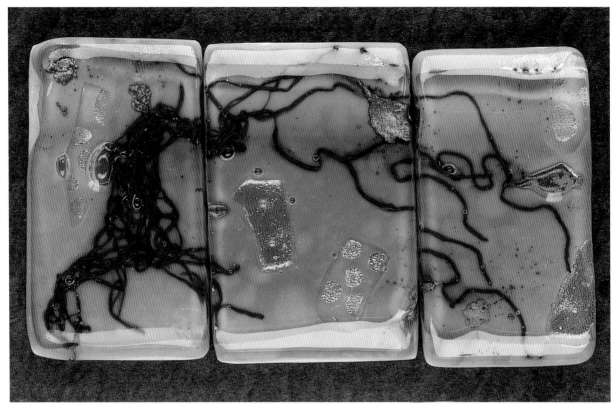

This was designed as part of a totem, for an exhibit at the Glass Artist's Fellowship Show at the Denver Botanical Gardens; the theme was the four seasons.

VILMA M. DALLAS
Autumn Triptych, 2002

Fused; cut; leaves, pearlescent powder, and copper; dichroic and fusible glass

5.7 x 9.5 x .6 cm

Photo by John Bonath, Mad Dog Studio

MONA LINDSEY GOLLAN
Talisman III, 2003

Lampworked; encased; stringer; hand-pulled cane; silver foil; soda-lime glass

3.7 x 1.6 cm

Photo by artist

TERI SOKOLOFF
Lava, 2003

Kilnformed; carved; dichroic and fusible glass; waxed linen cord

5.7 x 2.5 cm

Photo by S. Sokoloff

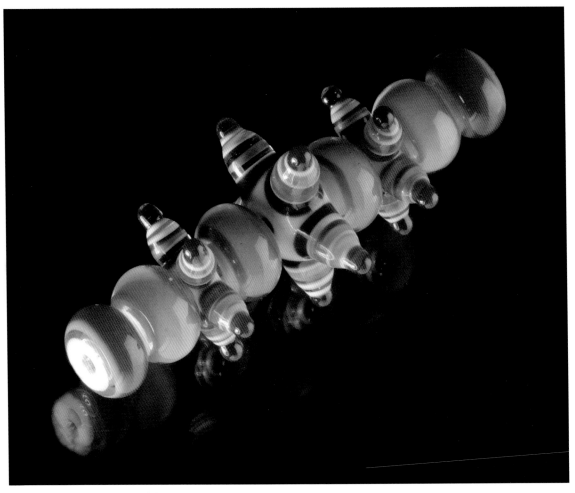

KIM VanANTWERP-POENISCH
Untitled, 2003

Lampworked; layered dots and stripes;
soda-lime glass

6 x 25 mm (focal bead)

Photo by Michael Kellet

FAITH WICKEY
Fishing for Fun, 2002

Lampworked; stringer; soda-lime
glass; wirework and pewter findings

5.7 x 5 x 1.3 cm

Photo by Jerry Anthony Photography

For me, the individual beads need to be part of a family—hence I make mostly jewelry.

PAMELA KAY WOLFERSBERGER
Deco Vessels, 2002

Lampworked; enamel; soda-lime glass; peridot, black onyx, crystal, and sterling accents

55 cm (necklace)

Photo by Jerry Anthony Photography

KAREN MOYER
Ladies Who Lunch, 2002

Lampworked; sculpted; soda-lime
glass

5 x 3.8 x 3.8 cm

Photo by Brian McLernon

LAVANA SHURTLIFF
Orange & Aqua Star Bracelet, 2003

Lampworked; stacked dots; soda-lime
glass; sterling silver findings

19 cm (bracelet)

Photo by Don Rutt

LILIANA CIRSTEA GLENN
I Stopped Drinking Coffee, 2003

Lampworked; encased; dots; stringer;
borosilicate glass; sterling silver accents

6.4 x 2.2 x .8 cm

Photo by Steve Gyurina

JERI CHANGAR
Ribbon Necklace, 2002

Lampworked; gold fumed; soda-lime
glass; sterling silver findings

40.6 cm (necklace)

Photo by David McCarthy

221

When I am not making beads I am usually thinking about making beads! I work in borosilicate glass because its high melting temperature allows me the reaction time that a 40-something-year old needs. I am also drawn to it for the colors I am able to achieve.

NANCY TOBEY
Untitled, 2001

Lampworked; encased; snipped; enamel; borosilicate glass

5.5 x 2 x 2 cm (largest bead)

Photo by Paul Avis

ALLISON JOHNSON
Beads, 2003

Lampworked; silver foil; soda-lime
glass; sterling silver end caps

2.2 x 3.8 x 2.2 cm (upper);
1.9 x 4.1 x 1.9 cm (lower)

Photo by Dan Grych

I used to collect rocks
as a kid. Now, I try to
make my own.

KIMBERLY JO AFFLECK
Cascade Opal, 2002

Flameworked; bicone; silver
fumed; partially encased;
soda-lime glass

4.4 x 1.9 cm

Photo by Roger Schreiber

I craft exotic, sculptural beads of substance. Formed with a hollow core, my beads are unplanned works that allow the glass to have its own voice.

JULIE WUEST
Heart of Gold, 1998

Lampworked; luster powder;
soda-lime glass

7.6 x 7 x 2.5 cm

Photo by Azad

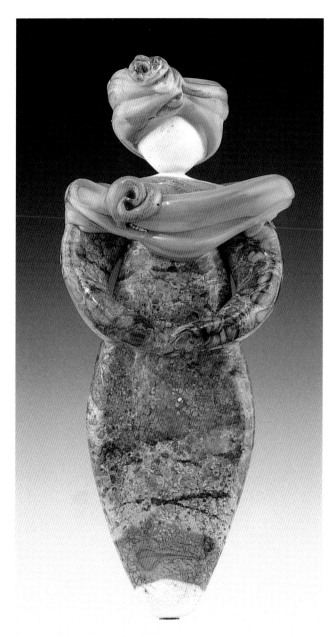

LOUISE LITTLE
Desert Blooms, 2003

Flameworked; curved tabular;
heavily encased; complex latticino;
silver foil; soda-lime glass

3 x 2.7 x 1.2 cm

Photo by artist

STEVI BELLE-DAVIDSON
Glass Gal—Colette, 2002

Flameworked; layered; sculpted; frit;
enamel; soda-lime glass

8 x 3.8 x 1.9 cm

Photo by Jerry Anthony Photography

JIMMY LOU JACKSON
Untitled, 2003

Lampworked; tabular; pulled stringer;
enamel; soda-lime glass; glass and
enamel accent beads, leather cord

3 x 1.2 cm (focal beads)

Photo by Terry Nelson

The swirl pattern is created by dragging a metal pick through colored stripes of glass on the surface of the bead. The bead is then cased in clear and sprayed with the iridizing solution while still hot.

BUDD MELLICHAMP
Orange and Yellow Iridized Swirl, 2001

Lampworked; encased; raked; iridized; soda-lime glass

3.8 x 2.4 cm

Photo by Rob Overton

The Cosmos beads are a metaphor for life. The form of the beads is consistent and predictable much like daily life; the design of the beads is a swirling mix with no beginning or ending.

BRENDAN BLAKE
Cosmos Series, 2003

Lampworked; blown; marbled; borosilicate glass tubing

3 x 2.4 cm (left); 3 x 2.3 cm (right)

Photo by Shauna Blake

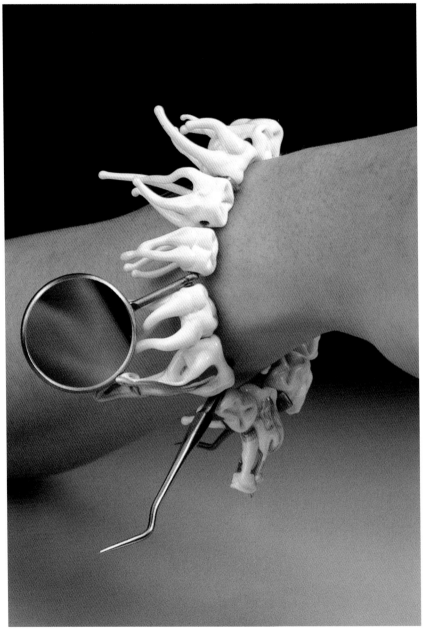

A desire to avoid the pain of cavities inspired this piece.

JENNIFER METTLEN NOLAN
Self Dental Exam, 2003

Lampworked; raked and pulled dots; soda-lime glass; stainless steel dental tools and findings

15.2 x 15.2 x 5 cm

Photo by Rob Glover

This bead is inspired by the walls of mines, with veins of metals, minerals, and other mysterious forms.

LOUISE MEHAFFEY
Lodestone, 2002

Lampworked; silver foil; reduction frit; soda-lime glass

5 x 2.6 x 1 cm

Photo by Jerry Anthony Photography

ALLISON LINDQUIST
Hawaiian Lei Necklace, 2001

Flameworked; layered poked dots; heavily
encased; soda-lime glass

45.7 cm (necklace); 1.9 cm (beads)

Photo by Don Tuttle

MARYBETH PICCIRELLI
Pixie Dust Filagree, 2003

Lampworked; stringer; soda-lime glass

2.5 x 2.2 cm (each bead)

Photo by Tim Thayer

These beads are inspired by my love of
fabrics and other textiles. I especially love
ethnic prints from around the world.

JOYCE ROOKS
Patterned Bead Necklace, 2003

Lampworked; twisted canes;
contrasting dots; soda-lime glass

50.8 cm (necklace)

Photo by Azad

Alien beads appear when too much
structure turns the mind into zero gravity.

DON MEADOWS
Alien Beads, 2003

Lampworked; dots; stringer;
frit; enamel; gold and silver leaf;
soda-lime glass

Dimensions vary

Photo by Shannon Brickey

RENÉE HOLOUBEK
Woodland Birth, 2003

Lampworked; tabular; silver foil;
dichroic and soda-lime glass

3.8 x 3.8 x 3.8 cm

Photo by Mike Bowden

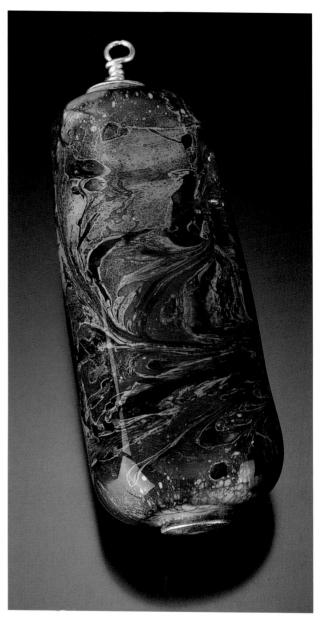

CHRIS DARLING-DᴇLISLE
The Tempest, 2003

Flameworked; encased; silver leaf
and goldstone; soda-lime glass

4.1 x 1.9 x 1.3 cm

Photo by R. Diamante, Portland, Maine

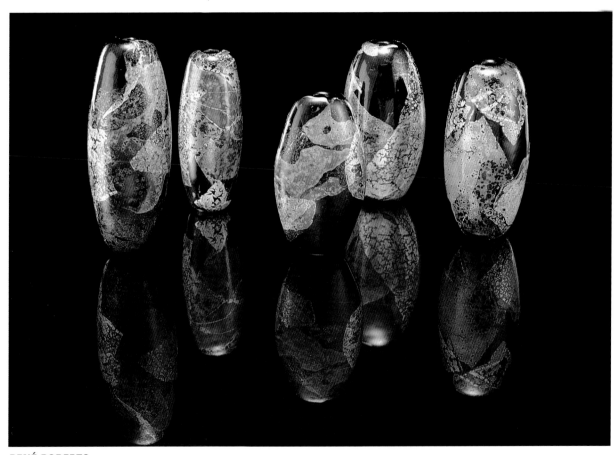

RENÉ ROBERTS
Black Beads from the Nebula Series,
1999–2001

Flameworked; blown glass shards; metal leaf (fine silver and 24k gold); soda-lime glass

5 cm (longest bead)

Photo by Hap Sakwa

Coming from an animation background, I like to tell stories and pay attention to detail.

LUCIE KOVAROVÁ
Octopus & Fish & Starfish, 2003

Lampworked; stringer; millefiori; layered; dichroic and soda-lime glass

3.5 x 3.2 x 3.3 cm

Photo by artist

Surrounded by exotic irises and orchids that grow near my Northern California home, I draw from nature to create my beads. This bead is from my multi-colored summer floral series.

LEAH FAIRBANKS
Faceted Multi-Floral, 2002

Lampworked; glass powders; gold and silver foil; copper mesh wire; soda-lime glass

Hand-faceted top by Derek Lusk

7.6 x 5.3 x 1.3 cm

Photo by Robert K. Liu

I love glass in all its facets. In the 23 years that I have been working with glass, there is constantly something new to discover.

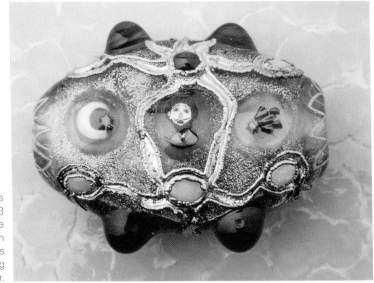

BRIAN KERKVLIET
Ruby Cosmic Bead, 1997

Flameworked; murrini; 24k electroforming: dichroic and soda-lime glass; opal and ruby stones

5 x 3.2 x 1.3 cm

Photo by artist

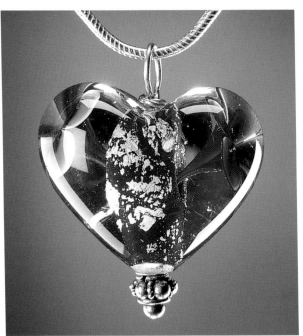

DAN BARNEY
Heart, 2003

Lampworked; encased; plunged; 22k-gold leaf; soda-lime glass

1.9 x 1.9 x 1.6 cm

Photo by Leon Woodward

DONALD JAY SCHNEIDER
Millefiori Pendants, 2002

Lampworked; encased millefiori; latticino edging; borosilicate glass

4.5 x 3 x 1 cm (each bead)

Photo by artist

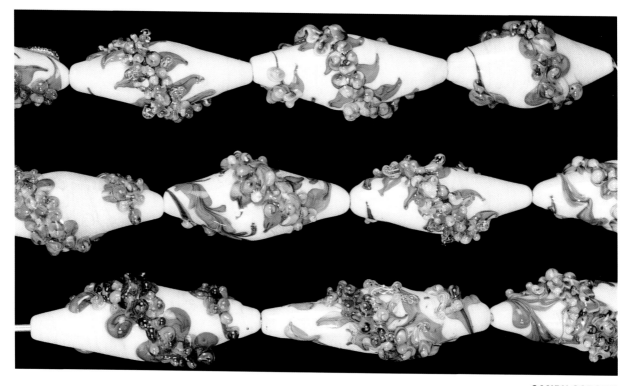

SANDY OSBORN
Wisteria Beads, 2002

Lampworked; bicone; encased
stringer; soda-lime glass

3.5 x 1.5 x 1.5 cm

Photo by Leslie Piña

HIROKO H. KOGURE
Untitled, 2003

Lampworked; dots; raked and pulled;
murrini; sandblasted; soda-lime glass

2.1 x 2.7 x 2.1 cm

Photo by artist

LESIA J. NULL
Black Bicones with Pink Flowers,
2003

Lampworked; layered; pulled stringer;
soda-lime glass

Dimensions vary

Photo by artist

My glass beads reflect my fascination with the magnifying quality of clear glass, as well as my passion for abstract art.

ELOISE COTTON
Abstract Beads, 1999

Lampworked; stringer; frit; shards; encased; borosilicate glass

Dimensions vary

Photo by Hap Sakwa

This piece was part of a series created specifically for The Maine Lakes Conservancy, Damariscotta, Maine.

CHRIS DARLING-DeLISLE
Spring Lake, 2003

Flameworked; hollow focal beads textured and flecked with gold leaf; focal and companion beads etched; soda-lime glass; 14k gold clasp and accent beads

45.7 cm (necklace)

Photo by R. Diamante, Portland, Maine

243

BECKY COOPER
Grape Urn, 2000

Lampworked; gold leaf; handmade
encased canes; soda-lime glass

4.8 x 2.5 x 2.5 cm

Photo by artist

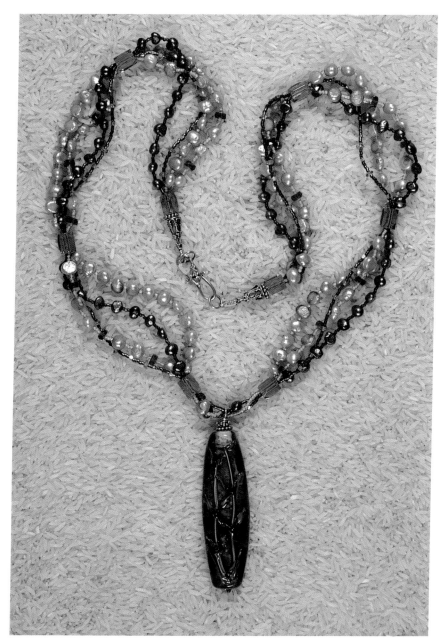

PATRICE BALLEW-ZUBILLAGA
Graceful Bamboo, 2002

Lampworked; encased; stringer; silver and gold foil; frit; dichroic and soda-lime glass; pearl, seed bead, and vintage glass accents, sterling silver findings

8.3 x 2.5 cm (focal bead)

Photo by artist

245

VICKIE WARBURTON
Dewdrops, 2003

Lampworked; raised and
twisted dots; soda-lime glass

3.8 x 1.5 cm (focal bead);
1.5 x .9 cm (accent beads)

Photo by Scott Flanagin

JENNIFER NAYLOR
Golden Rainbows, 2002

Flameworked; encased; gold leaf;
rainbow cane; soda-lime glass;
gold-filled wire bead accents

7.6 x 8.9 cm

Photo by Margo Geist

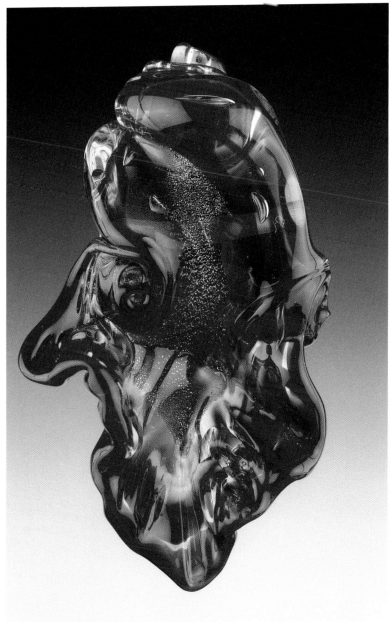

ANN SHERM BALDWIN
Underwater Fire, 2002

Lampworked; sculpted; dichroic
and soda-lime glass

7.6 x 3.2 x 2.5 cm

Photo by Jerry Anthony Photography

In my work I challenge myself to create unique objects from glass and metal.

KATHRYN WARDILL
Carved Bead Neckpiece, 2000

Flameworked; hollow; handcarved; soda-lime glass; oxidized silver elements and handmade clasp

22 x 3 x 3 cm (necklace)

Photo by artist

PATRICIA ZABRESKI VENALECK
Chinese Red, 2003

Lampworked; stringer; soda-lime glass; crystal
and silver spacers, sterling silver toggle clasp

45.7 cm (necklace); 3 x 3.1 cm (focal bead)

Photo by Patrick Buschmohle

KRISTINA LOGAN
Collection of Beads, 2003
Lampworked; soda-lime glass
7.3 cm (largest bead)
Photo by Paul Avis

KIM MANCHESTER
Necklace, 2000

Lampworked; layered; stringer;
dichroic soda-lime glass; handmade
silver charms

76.2 cm (necklace);
3.8 x 1.9 cm (largest bead)

Photo by Carl Tamura

BARBARA K. HOLLOSY
Santa Fe, 2003

Lampworked; hollow; encased; soda-lime glass

5 x 3.8 cm

Photo by Larry Saunders

I use traditional glassblowing techniques that focus on color and form. I love the enduring nature of glass, its timeless quality, and unending possibilities.

CONNIE S. SULLIVAN
Black-n-Blue, 2002

Lampworked; encased twisted stringer; dots; soda-lime glass; sterling silver and anodized aluminum wire

61 cm (necklace); 2.5 cm (largest bead)

Photo by Don Rutt

A modern version of the evil eye, Freeks ward off weirdness and negativity.

CARYN WALSH
Freeks!, 2003

Flameworked; gravity-formed;
surface decoration of stringer
and dots; soda-lime glass

Dimensions vary

Photo by David S. Orr

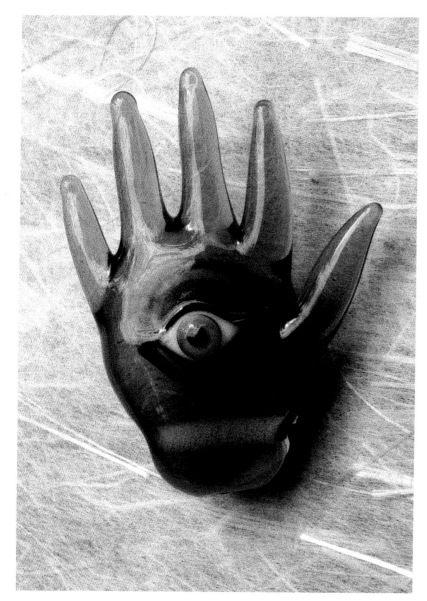

The hand is our most precious tool in doing glass. The eye represents the evil eye to ward off evil. The spiral represents the continuum of life.

WILLIAM C. STOKES III
Handing It to You, 2003

Lampworked; sculpted; aventurine; soda-lime glass

5 x 2.5 x .6 cm

Photo by artist

255

I am most inspired by repeating patterns and symmetrical forms in nature. Peas lined up in a pod, caterpillars, egg casings, diatoms and protozoa, seed pods and starfish; all these things interest me, and I find stylized elements of these forms emerging in my beads.

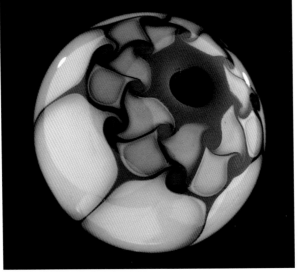

TERRI CASPARY SCHMIDT
Segmented Amber Pod, 2000

Lampworked; layered; twisted-dot end details; soda-lime glass

2.1 x 2.5 cm

Photo by David Egan Photography

KATHY JOHNSON
Universe, 2003

Lampworked; handmade murrini; silver foil and leaf; fine silver; soda-lime glass

1.9 x 6 x 1.9 cm

Photo by Roger Schreiber

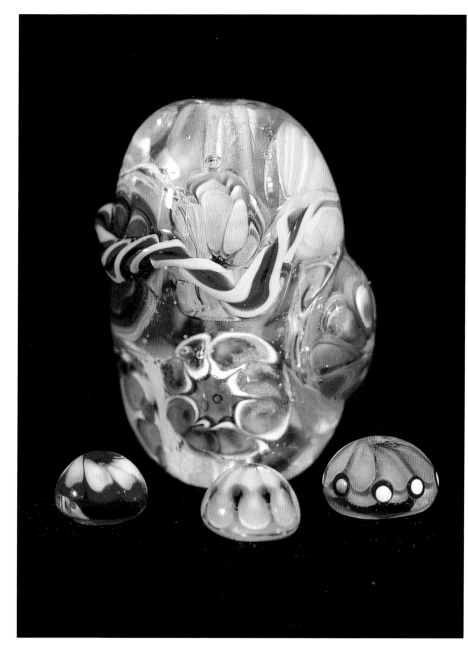

The "gizmos" are like small anemones or jellyfish. Each gizmo is a separately lamp-worked component made of layers of colored glass dots.

BUDD MELLICHAMP
Seaform #22, 2003

Lampworked; layered dots; raised features; twistie; soda-lime glass

3.8 x 2.5 x 2.5 cm

Photo by Richard Brunck

**NANCY KAUMEYER
HERRINGTON**
Red Tide, 2002

Lampworked; fumed; latticino;
reduction frit; goldstone;
pearlescent powder; stringer;
silver foil; soda-lime glass

4.1 x 2.2 x 2.2 cm

Photo by Jerry Anthony Photography

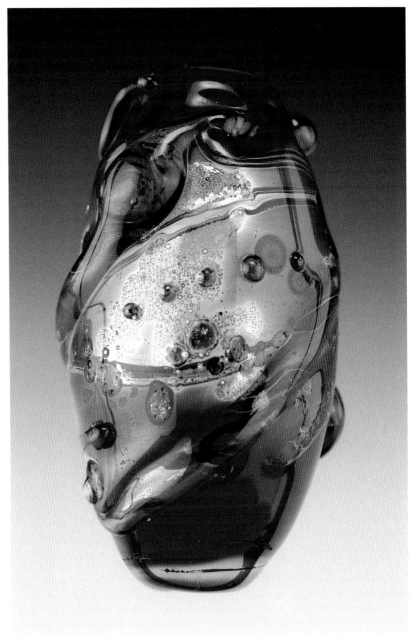

This necklace was inspired by the
beads of China's Warring States period.

NICOLE CARLSON
Warrior Necklace, 2003

Lampworked; stacked dot decoration in
Warring States style; soda-lime glass

Dimensions vary

Photo by Robbyn Gordon

After a year of experimentation, I was able to find a good combination of torch and glass types to compose the orchid form.

MONTY CLARK
Orchid Bead, 2003

Lampworked; sculpted; dichroic and soda-lime glass

7 x 4.4 x 1.9 cm

Photo by Keith Sutter

I made the bead in the clasp, and spent much time developing a clasp system that is easy to work and integrates well with glass bead jewelry.

KATE ROTHRA
The Caterpillar, 2003

Lampworked; layered color; dichroic and soda-lime glass

49.5 cm (necklace)

Photo by George Post

I love color and pattern. I was a toy designer and I worked in the fashion industry as a fabric designer and color stylist. Now I own a gallery and raise exotic chickens. I love that my beads make people smile.

JENNIFER FIELD MILLER
Goddess & Chicken Totems, 2002

Lampworked; dots; stringer; soda-lime glass; forged steel and copper bases

10.2 cm (tallest bead)

Photo by Rennie Newmark

KIMBERLY JO AFFLECK
Heartwood, 2003

Flameworked; bicone; silver fumed;
soda-lime glass

10.8 x 1.3 cm

Photo by Roger Schreiber

MARY H. KARG
Guardian Spirit VII, 2002

Lampworked; stringer; silver leaf; acid etched;
soda-lime glass; vintage feathers, porcupine
quills, leather and fabric

30.5 x 7.6 x 5 cm

Photo by Jerry Anthony Photography

263

Pure joy is collaborating with my husband. The warmth of the wood and the coolness of the glass are seductive. The candlestick is a celebration of our island home.

MICHELLE WILMAN
Two for Tea, 2002

Flameworked; shaped; poked and twisted dots; raked stripes; soda-lime glass

Maple base and top by Robert Wilman

17.8 x 10.2 cm

Photo by Tammy Lee Photographics

SCOTT ROSINSKI
Inside-Out Spirals, 2003

Lampworked; inside-out technique;
borosilicate glass tubing

5 x 2.5 x 5 cm (largest bead)

Photo by R. Diamante, Portland, Maine

After making beads for five years I decided to try something new—enamels. The color combinations are endless and the reaction when heated creates these great watercolor effects.

SHER BERMAN
Extreme Enamels, 2003

Flameworked; layered enamel powder; boiled; heat polished; soda-lime glass

3.2 x 2.5 cm (left); 4.4 x 1.9 cm (right)

Photo by Greg Kuepfer

The pieces are inspired by my love of antique glass and vessel forms. I love the reaction when I tell people the finish is from "a secret, special chemical formula"—baking soda!

PRISCILLA TURNER SPADA
Antique Vessel Beads, 2002–03

Lampworked; enamel; soda-lime glass; copper handles; baking soda finish

3.2 x 3.8 x 1.9 cm (largest bead)

Photo by Pierre Chiha

267

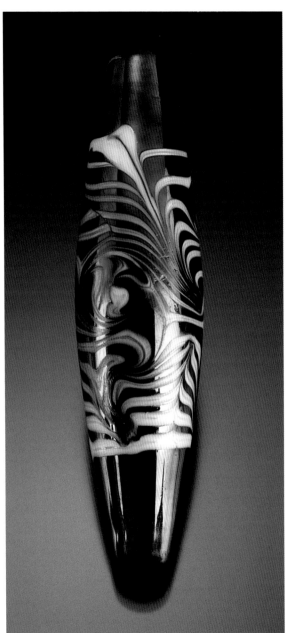

CAROL BUGARIN
Untitled, 2003

Lampworked; bicone; iridized;
soda-lime glass

5.7 x 1.3 cm

Photo by R. Diamante, Portland, Maine

I love deep, rich color;
layering gives me new
colors, shapes, and depth.

MICHELLE WALDREN
*Ribbon Cane Disk and
Teardrop,* 2003

Flameworked; layered; ribbon
cane; soda-lime glass

8.9 x 2.5 cm (left);
7.6 x 7.6 cm (right)

Photo by Roger Shrieber

NANCY TOBEY
Red and Blue Trapezoids, 2003

Lampworked; shaped;
borosilicate glass

4.5 x 3 x 1.5 cm (largest bead)

Photo by Paul Avis

LAURA L. BOWKER
Pathways, 2003

Lampworked; silver foil; soda-lime glass

3.3 x 2.5 x 1.2 cm (largest bead)

Photo by Roger Schreiber

The inspiration for these beads were the fruits and flowers I remember from my grandparents' garden.

KIM FIELDS
Fruits and Flowers, 2002

Lampworked; sculpted; striped and ribbon canes; encased stringers; stacked and raked dots; special color mixed bases; soda-lime glass

3.2 x 1.6 x 1.6 cm (focal beads);
1 x 1.2 x 1.2 cm (accent beads)

Photo by Tom Van Eynde

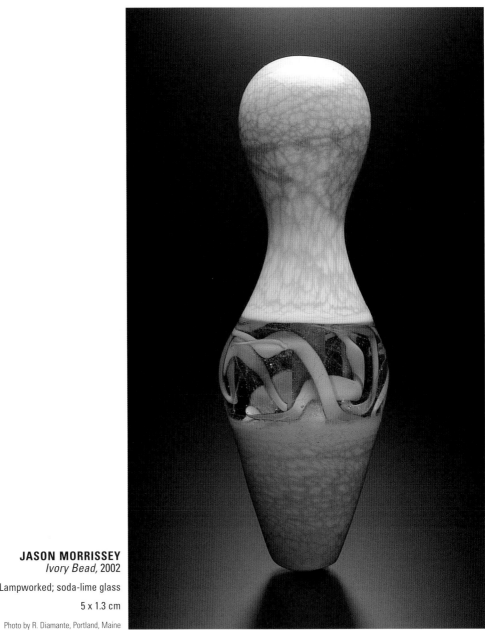

JASON MORRISSEY
Ivory Bead, 2002

Lampworked; soda-lime glass

5 x 1.3 cm

Photo by R. Diamante, Portland, Maine

Most of my bead designs involve variations on the simple but versatile technique of dot application. I like to watch patterns and shapes evolve naturally from the placement of dots and lines as they melt into the surface of the bead.

TERRI CASPARY SCHMIDT
Birds, 2003

Lampworked; dots; raked; masked; stringer; soda-lime glass

2.8 x 2 cm

Photo by David Egan Photography

TERRI CASPARY SCHMIDT
Untitled, 2003

Lampworked; layered and manipulated dots; stringer; soda-lime glass

4.6 x 2.1 cm

Photo by David Egan Photography

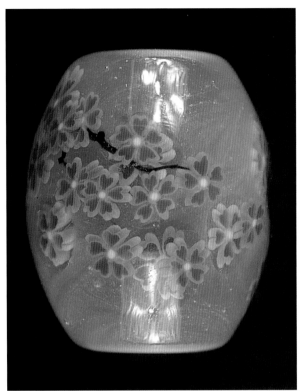

AKIHIRO OHKAMA
Cherry Blossom, 2001

Lampworked; murrini; soda-lime glass

2.5 x 2 x 2 cm

Photo by Youichi Sueyoshi

EMIKO NUMATA
Easter Egg, 2001

Lampworked; handmade
millefiori; dots; lead glass

2.5 x 2.2 x 2.2 cm

Photo by MGM (JAPAN)

YASUHIRO OHKAMA
Japanese Castle, 1990

Lampworked; murrini;
soda-lime glass

2 x 2 x 2 cm

Photo by Youichi Sueyoshi

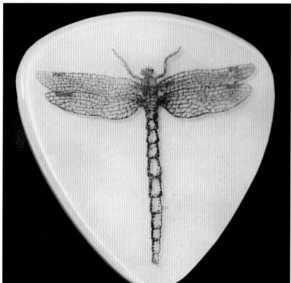

KAREN KAY VELARDE
Timeless Dragonfly, 2003

Fused; fiber-paper formed bead
hole; sifted enamels; ground and
polished; silkscreen from original
drawing; fusible glass

7.6 x 7.2 x 1.1 cm

Photo by Barry L. Velarde

I create my pieces with glass, but also have an obsession for stones. So...I love to make glass that has the look and feel of stone.

JEN ZITKOV
Finding Bliss, 2003

Lampworked; engraved; soda-lime glass; sterling silver, denim lapis, garnet, and tiger-eye accents

50.8 cm (necklace);
5.7 x 2.5 x .6 cm (focal bead)

Photo by artist

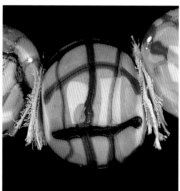

TAMARA MELCHER
Glad Plaid, 2002

Torchworked; hollow; fluorite bead
accents and silk organza spacers

18.4 x 10.2 x 1.6 cm (necklace)

Photo by David Egan Photography

With a background as an electrical engineer, I have developed a sense of intricate patterns and geometry combined with simplicity of form, which you will see in each bead I make. My passion is the colors, the play of light on the glass and metals, all created with a sense of fun that I want to see reflected in each piece of art I create.

DEBRA K. WELLS
Colorado Charm, 2003

Lampworked; stringer; dots; soda-lime glass; sterling silver and charm

19 cm (bracelet)

Photo by Azad

ANITA SPENCER
Bracelet (9 Dot Beads), 2002

Lampworked; soda-lime glass;
silver accents

27 cm (bracelet)

Photo by Jerry Anthony Photography

BEVERLY D. HOWARD
Untitled, 2003

Lampworked; sculpted; formed
and kiln-fired metal clay; cubic
zirconia; soda-lime glass

5 x 2.1 x 2.2 cm

Photo by David S. Orr

279

KAREN KAY VELARDE
Geisha with Fan, 2003

Fused; fiber-paper formed bead hole; etched;
painted; fired twice; ground and polished;
fusible glass

7.4 x 7.4 x .9 cm

Photo by Barry L. Velarde

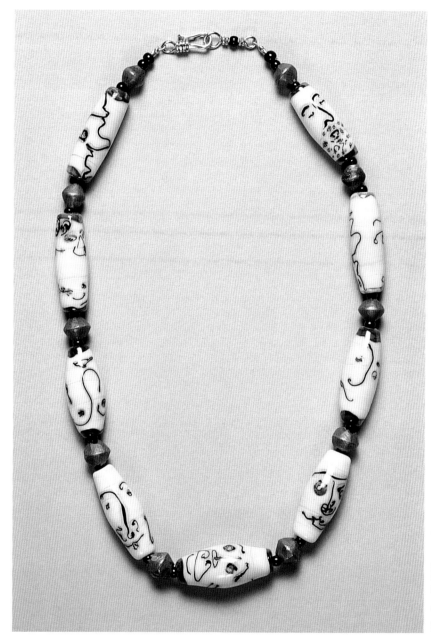

Using fine stringers on beads is tricky, as they melt too easily. The face designs on my beads are a collaboration between my hand and the flame, and some of the characters who show up are not the ones I planned to invite.

CONNIE POLLARD
Good Company, 2003

Lampworked; stringer; soda-lime glass; brass and bead accents, handmade sterling silver wire clasp

47 cm (necklace); 3.5 x 1.6 cm (beads)

Photo by Susan Byrne Photography

281

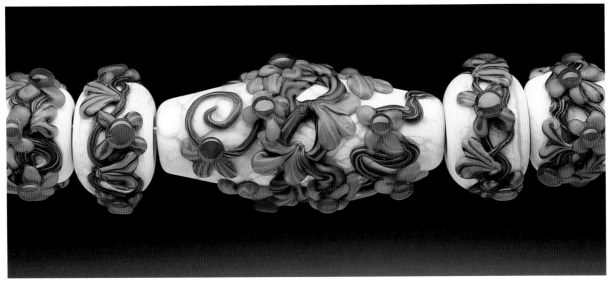

KIM FIELDS
Bittersweet Vines, 2002

Lampworked; partially etched;
striped cane and encased stringers;
soda-lime glass

3.3 x 1.6 x 1.6 cm (focal bead);
1 x 1.3 x 1.3 cm (accent beads)

Photo by Tom Van Eynde

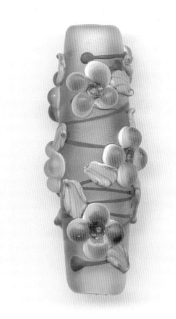

SARA HOYT
Lush, 2003

Lampworked; threaded stringer; layered
and pushed dots; patterned cane; handbuilt murrini; etched; soda-lime glass

3.5 x 1.5 x 1.5 cm

Photo by artist

KALEIGH HESSEL
Rain Forest Lost, 2003

Flameworked; latticino; complex and
reduction stringer; soda-lime glass

3.6 x 2.5 x 1 cm (largest bead)

Photo by Seth Tice-Lewis

My work centers on magic and fantasy. This piece is one of a series of figures, each holding a crystal ball that includes a slice of canework.

MAVIS SMITH
Dark Lady, 2003

Lampworked; sculpted; hand-made murrini; soda-lime glass

5.7 x 3.8 x 3.2 cm

Photo by artist

GLADYS J. BAEZ-DICKREITER
Garden Friends, 2002–03

Lampworked; sculpted; surface decoration of dots,
stringer, and handmade cane; soda-lime glass

3.5 x 2.5 x 1 cm (largest bead)

Photo by artist

SHERRY PLOOF
Eden's Villain, 2002

Lampworked; silver foil; fine silver; goldstone;
soda-lime glass; freshwater pearls, sterling
silver, and seed bead accents

61 cm (necklace); 1 x 1.6 cm (focal bead)

Photo by R. Diamante, Portland, Maine

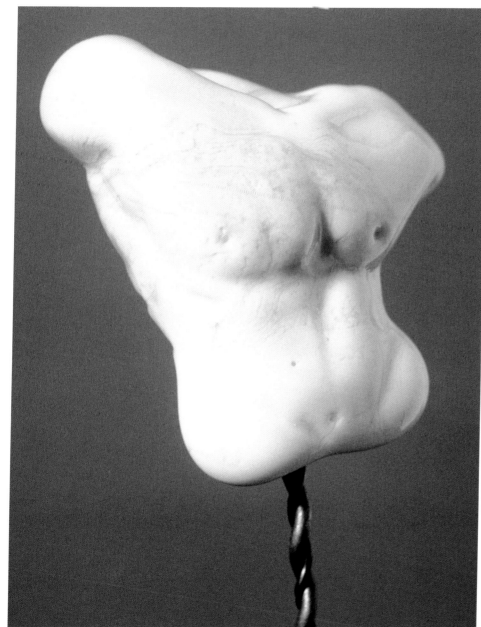

I love making the
monumental in miniature.

**PRISCILLA TURNER
SPADA**
Classical Torso Bead, 2000
Lampworked; soda-lime glass
2.9 x 2.9 x 1.3 cm
Photo by Pierre Chiha

BERNADETTE SCARANI MAHFOOD
Helix Pendant, 2002

Flameworked beads, kilnformed pendant; dichroic and soda-lime glass; helix bead weaving, handmade sterling silver chain

17.8 x 8.3 x 1.3 cm

Photo by Larry Sanders

PATTI WOOD WHITELEY
Dichroic Donut, 2003

Kilnformed; fused; dichroic and fusible glass

5 x 6.4 cm

Photo by Steve Meltzer

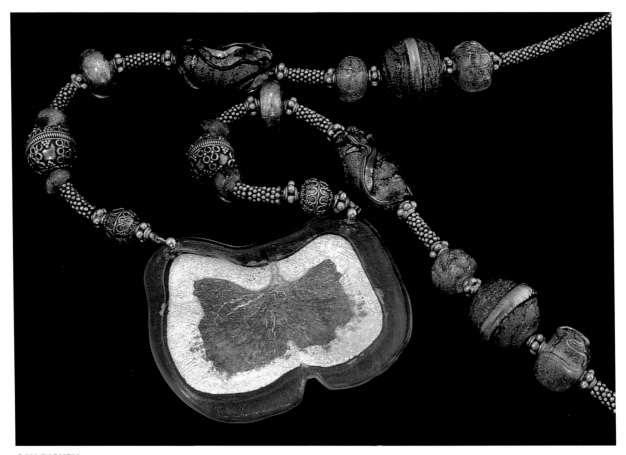

CAY DICKEY
Fused Ginko Leaf & Dichroic Beads, 2003

Flameworked; dichroic and soda-lime glass; silver spacers

3.8 x 5.7 cm (pendant)

Photo by Carl Tamura

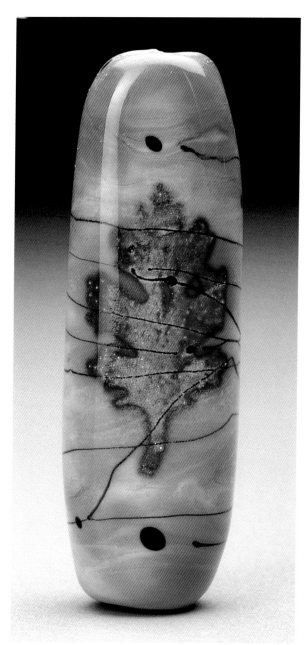

INGRID HEIN
Leaves of Glass, 2002

Lampworked; silver foil; soda-lime glass

5 x 1.6 cm

Photo by Roger Schreiber

TERI SOKOLOFF
Tiki, 2003

Kilnformed; carved; dichroic and fusible
glass; waxed linen cord and silver beads

5 x 1.9 cm

Photo by S. Sokoloff

LESLIE THIEL
Fused Watchband Beads, 2001

Kilnformed; applied decal; fused; shaped; drilled;
fire polished; slumped; fusible glass

5 x 1.9 x .6 cm (each bead)

Photo by Roger Schreiber

CALVIN G. ORR
Lavender Blue, 2003

Lampworked; hand-pulled cane; encased; soda-lime glass

1.5 x 2 cm (focal bead)

Photo by Joey Nakamura

These are my favorite, and most difficult, beads to make. Each bead is treated like a canvas.

JOHN WINTER
Enamel Beads, 2003

Lampworked; trailed; raked; etched; metal foils; enamel; soda-lime glass

4.4 x 1.9 x .9 cm

Photo by Tommy Olof Elder

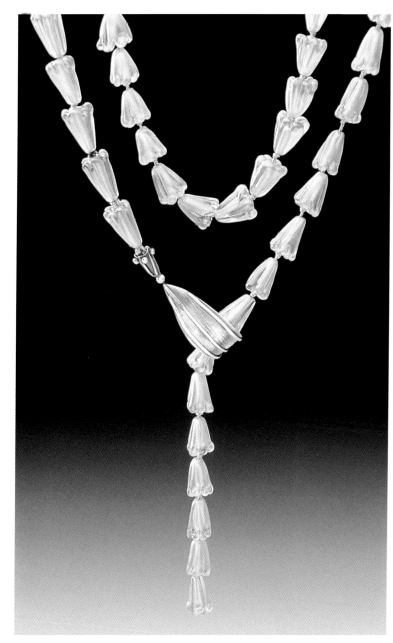

PATTI DOUGHERTY
Lotus Necklace, 2003

Lampworked; pearlescent enamel; soda-lime glass; hand-forged sterling silver clasp

81.3 x 1.9 x 1.9 cm (necklace)

Photo by Peter Groesbeck

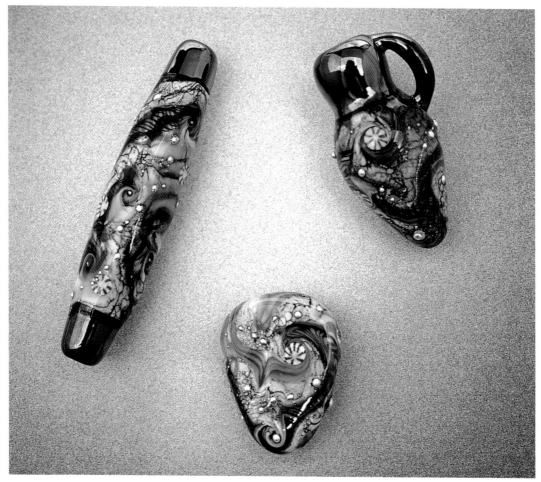

SHIRLEY COOK
Bronze Age Suite, 2003

Lampworked; latticino; millefiori; silvered ivory;
fine silver; reduction frit; soda-lime glass

7.6 x 1.7 cm (largest bead)

Photo by Len Cook

KRISTINA LOGAN
Ivory Disk Bead, 2003

Lampworked; soda-lime glass

1.3 x 5.4 x 5.4 cm

Photo by Paul Avis

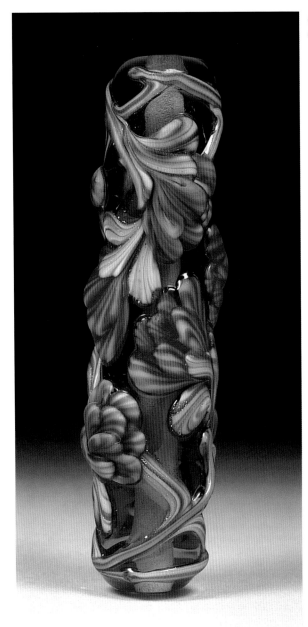

Color is the essence of my work, just as it is the essence of our perception of the natural world.

I love the reaction to my encased florals. People are always asking, "But how do you get the flowers in there?"

PEGGY ROSE
Daffodils in Spring, 2002

Lampworked; encased; soda-lime glass

2.5 x 2.5 x 2.5 cm

Photo by artist

KRISTEN FRANTZEN ORR
Floral Tapestry, 2002

Lampworked; etched; layered and striped canes; soda-lime glass

5.7 x 1.3 x 1.3 cm

Photo by David Orr

MICHEALE GORDON
Bead Collection, 2003

Flameworked; plunged; raked; handmade cane;
raised dots; silver foil; soda-lime glass

2.4 cm (largest bead)

Photo by Kevin McHone

I like the humorous aspect of life-sized ants crawling on the surface of a bead. The very formal design format opposes the whimsy, I think.

BARBARA BECKER SIMON
Ant Bead Group, 2003

Lampworked; dots; stringer; twistie; soda-lime glass

Dimensions vary

Photo by Rob Stegmann

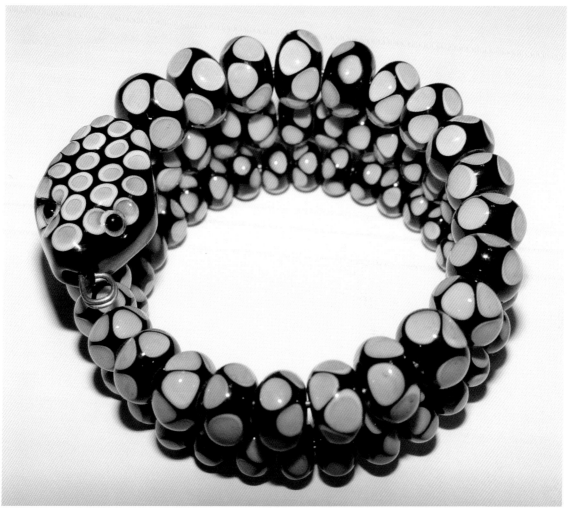

JERRI ROEY
Snake Bracelet, 2001

Lampworked; dots; soda-lime
glass; memory wire

53 cm (bracelet)

Photo by Craig Armstrong

301

I've always loved the visual magic of glass: the illusions its transparency, magnification, and refraction create. The layering and manipulation I do behind the torch may create the physical petals, tendrils, and leaves, but these qualities of the glass itself bring them to life.

KIM WERTZ
Three Springtime Florals, 2003

Lampworked; layered; encased; dichroic base; soda-lime glass

4.8 x 2 cm (largest bead)

Photo by Greg Galardy

DEANNA GRIFFIN DOVE
*Winter Meadow
(Meadow Series),* 2002

Flameworked; surface decoration of stringer and striped cane; dichroic and soda-lime glass

3.2 x 1.9 x 1.9 cm

Photo by artist

LOUISE LITTLE
Desert Flowers, 2003

Flameworked; bicone; encased; complex latticino;
silver and gold foil; soda-lime glass

4 x 1.8 x 1.8 cm

Photo by artist

I enjoy making glass beads with abstract, painterly qualities. Inspiration comes from landscapes, art and artifacts, Asian design. I like pieces that are quiet yet complex.

LOUISE MEHAFFEY
Lichen, 2003

Lampworked; copper and silver leaf; reduction frit; enamels; soda-lime glass

4.3 x 3.3 x 1 cm

Photo by Tom Weigand Studio

CYNTHIA LIEBLER SAARI
Passion, 2002

Lampworked; reduction powder; enamel; soda-lime glass

3.2 x 3.2 cm

Photo by Ralph Gabriner

MARJORIE BURR
Emergence, 2003

Lampworked; encased; dots; electroformed and
patinaed copper; dichroic and soda-lime glass

2.7 x 1.6 x 1.6 cm

Photo by Roger Schreiber

KRISTEN FRANTZEN ORR
Japanese Silk, 2003

Lampworked; gold leaf inclusions; partially etched; handmade multi-layered striped cane; soda-lime glass

Necklace design and beadwork by Maggie Roschyk

3.8 x 3.8 x 1.6 cm

Photo by David Orr

CATHY KAYE
Eye Candy, 2003

Lampworked; tabular; dichroic and
soda-lime glass; vintage bead accents

61 x 1.3 x .6 cm (necklace)

Photo by artist

I like to use several different patterns and colors of dichroic glass to create depth in my beads.

LISA ST. MARTIN
Sunset, 2002

Lampworked; dichroic glass inclusions; soda-lime glass

3.8 x 2.5 x 2.5 cm

Photo by Jerry Anthony Photography

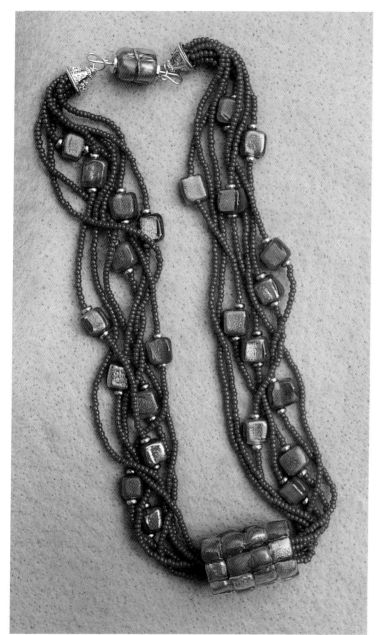

NORMA SHAPIRO
Patchwork Quilt Necklace, 2003

Flameworked; applied patches; dichroic and
soda-lime glass; flameworked bead clasp and
companion beads with seed bead accents

45.7 cm (necklace); 1.9 x 3.2 x 1.9 cm (focal bead)

Photo by artist

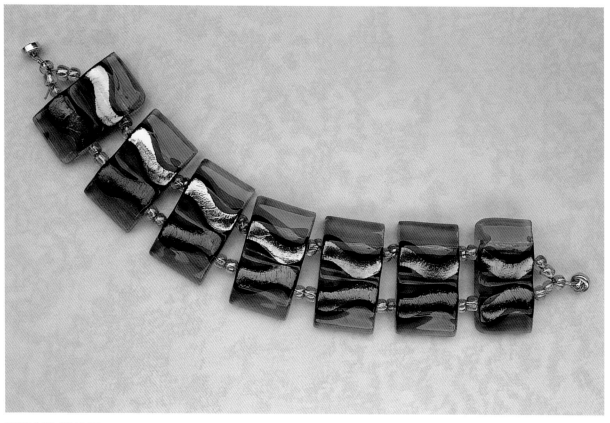

VILMA M. DALLAS
Midas Touched, 2003

Fused; cut; dichroic and fusible glass

3.2 x 16.5 x .9 cm

Photo by John Bonath, Mad Dog Studio

MARCIA J. PARKER
Hollow Beads: Gold Leaf Heart and Urchin Dot, 2003

Lampworked; hollow; raised dots; gold leaf and aventurine; soda-lime glass

2.9 x 2.2 x 2.9 cm (left); 2.5 x 2.2 x 2.2 cm (right)

Photo by Kallan Nishimoto

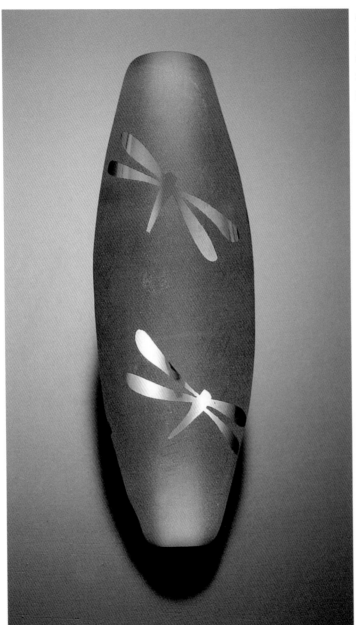

ALETHIA DONATHAN
Sand Carved Series, 2003

Lampworked; gold fumed;
sandblasted; soda-lime glass

3.2 x 1.3 cm

Photo by Azad

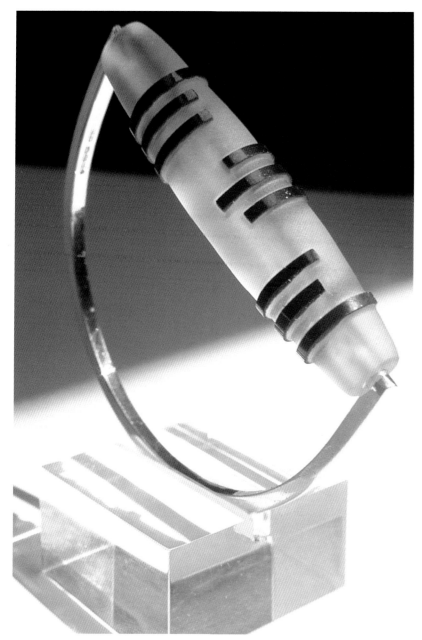

DIANA EAST
Bars Bangle, 2002

Flameworked; enamel; sandblasted;
soda-lime glass; sterling silver mount

5.7 x 6.4 x 1.3 cm

Photo by artist

DAVID AND REBECCA JURGENS
Ancient One, 2003

Flameworked; sculpted; coil potting;
raised frit; soda-lime glass; sterling,
moonstone, and crystal accents

7.6 x 3.8 x 2.5 cm

Photo by Rebecca Jurgens

DEBBIE CROWLEY
Coral Reef Specimen Series, 2003

Lampworked; sculpted; gold fumed; frit; enamel; reduction powder; soda-lime glass; borosilicate glass stands

17.8 x 45.7 x 15.2 cm

Photo by Harold Wood

MAVIS SMITH
Faery, 2003

Lampworked; twisted stringer; handmade encased murrini; dichroic and soda-lime glass

7 x 7 x 1.9 cm

Photo by artist

315

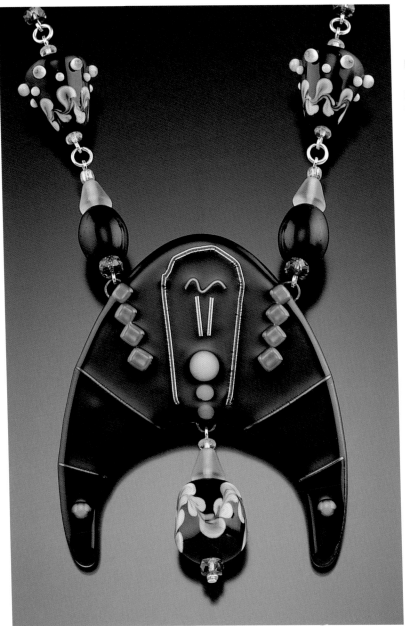

BERNADETTE SCARANI MAHFOOD
Tunis Revisited, 2002

Flameworked beads, kilnformed pendant; dichroic and soda-lime glass; handmade sterling silver chain

15.2 x 7.6 x 1.9 cm

Photo by Larry Sanders

Tucked away safely in a small and tattered leather drawstring pouch are my treasured "hippie beads" from my time in San Francisco in the 1960s. I was a teenager then. It's over 40 years later, and I am still under the spell of those beads as a member of an artistic movement of people who are lovingly and passionately creating beads unlike any that have ever existed.

INARA KNIGHT
Garden of My Mind, 2002

Flameworked; tabular; frit and dichroic inclusions; surface trailing; soda-lime glass

5.7 x 3.8 x .9 cm (largest bead)

Photo by Jeff O'Dell

317

As artists and as people we are often asked to place ourselves in categories. I'm a "Suess-ian." I believe in absurdities and three impossible things before breakfast and a person is a person no matter how small.

ROBIN WYMAN FOSTER
Primarily Suessian, 2003

Lampworked; selenium- and copper-reaction formed lines; cane techniques; soda-lime glass

4 cm (largest bead)

Photo by David Orr

A friend once said that I have a knack for putting together weird colors and making the combination look good.

PATTI L. CAHILL
2003 Collection, 2002–03

Lampworked; dots; raked; pulled; handmade millefiore; stringers; handmade mixed colors; soda-lime glass

Dimensions vary

Photo by artist

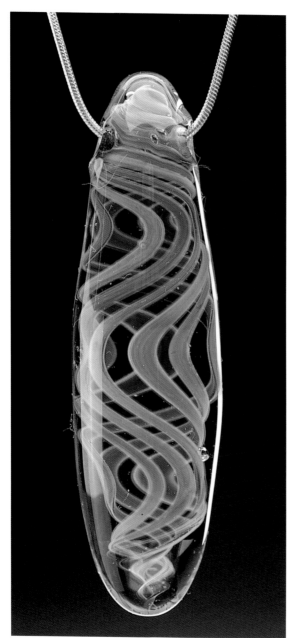

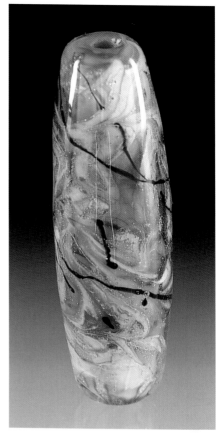

KALEIGH HESSEL
Desert Sunset Focal, 2003

Flameworked; layered; encased;
fine silver foil; soda-lime glass

4.6 x 1.4 cm

Photo by Seth Tice-Lewis

ELLIE BURKE
Solid Reversal Pendant, 2002

Flameworked; filigrana; reverse twist; borosilicate
glass tubing; sterling silver chain

6.4 x 1.9 x 1.9 cm

Photo by William F. Lemke

Oddly shaped broken pieces of glass
suggest landscapes that I build upon;
in the heat of the kiln they magically
turn into their own small worlds.

LAURIE SHAW
Fused Glass Landscapes, 2003

Kilnformed; fused; layered; coldworked;
dichroic and fusible glass

7.6 x 7.6 x .6 cm (largest bead)

Photo by Tommy Olof Elder

CAROL J. FONDA
Flower Pendant, 2003

Lampworked; sculpted; dichroic
and soda-lime glass

5.4 x 3.8 x 1.6 cm

Photo by Keith Sutter

One of my teachers in the early 1990s was Michael Max; I liked his raked eye bead but wanted it turned around. When I re-oriented the design to the hole and flattened it, I found a new shape I could call my own—the Maltese Star.

JENNY NEWTSON
Maltese Star #36, 2002

Lampworked; layered; raked; palladium foil; soda-lime glass; sterling silver accents

3.2 x 4.4 x 1.3 cm

Photo by Daniel Van Rossen

This murrina has six components (eye, nose, mouth, ear, earring, and rose) which were assembled hot in the flame of a torch. The assembling took nearly five hours before it was ready to pull.

ISIS RAY
Frida Kahlo Bead, 2002

Flameworked; murrina; gold leaf; soda-lime glass

3.8 x 2.9 x .9 cm

Photo by Roger Schreiber

BRIAN KERKVLIET
Cosmic Dreamscape, 2001

Flameworked; murrini; 24k electroforming:
dichroic and soda-lime glass; opal and
ruby stones

6.4 x 3.8 x 1.3 cm

Photo by artist

ALETHIA DONATHAN
Painted Desert, 2002

Lampworked; silver foil; acid etched;
soda-lime glass

Necklace design and beadwork by
Joanne Strehle Bast

35.6 x 6.4 x 2.5 cm (necklace);
1.9 cm (focal bead)

Photo by Jerry Anthony Photography

MORGANE GUILCHER
Untitled, 2003

Lampworked; fused; soda-lime glass;
steel cable and sterling silver clasps

45.7 x 6.4 x 5 cm (necklace)

Photo by Paul Fournier

My artistic goal is to instill a sense of happiness and intrigue in those who see my beads and wear them. The piece realizes its ultimate completion only when it and its wearer come together. Though I'm largely self-taught, Tom Holland and Patricia Sage have been my mentors and influenced my bead art.

MARKELS LORINI
Turquoise with Leaf Swirl Design Bead & Sterling Bracelet, 2003

Flameworked; tabular; raked dots; dichroic and soda-lime glass; sterling silver accents

20.3 cm (bracelet); 1.9 x 2.5 x .7 cm (beads)

Photo by Ralph Gabriner

LANI CHING
Untitled Necklace, 2001

Flameworked; dots and twisted dots;
soda-lime glass

66 cm (necklace); 3.2 cm (focal bead)

Photo by Teresa Sullivan

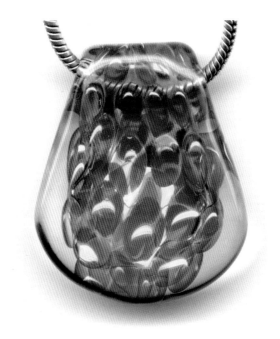

In this process I apply layers of vapors from precious metals and colored glass to the inside of the bead, then it is reduced and shaped. This gives the piece an amazing depth and brings the inside to life! The pieces are also fully annealed and signed...no two pieces are ever alike.

CHAD PITTS
Golden Rain, 2003

Blown; inside-out technique; precious metals; reduced and shaped; borosilicate glass

3.2 x 2.5 x .9 cm

Photo by artist

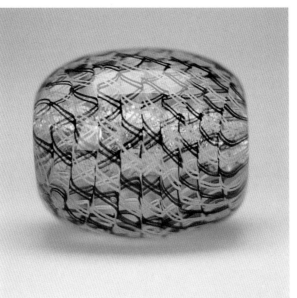

NORIKAZU KOGURE
Tonbodama, 2003

Lampworked; gold leaf; soda-lime glass

2.5 cm

Photo by artist

BONNIE HARDER
Assorted Flavors, 2003

Lampworked; hollow; soda-lime glass

1.5 x 1.8 cm

Photo by Chris Petrauskas

CAITLIN B. HYDE
Four Flameworked Beads, 2000

Flameworked; surface pattern techniques;
marvered; soda-lime glass

5.7 x 1.3 x 1.3 cm (each bead)

Photo by artist

I'm fascinated with glass and beadmaking.
I'm constantly exploring the limitations and
the possibilities of glass which result in
many failed experiments and more
beautiful surprises.

MARTHA GIBERSON
Tribute, 2000

Flameworked; hollow; stringer; soda-lime
glass; sterling silver beads

61 x 3.8 cm (necklace)

Photo by Steve Gyurina

I stacked and arranged these beads to give
the impression of a group of folk standing
and talking together—a bead village group.

APRIL ZILBER
Bead Village, 1998

Lampworked; silver foil;
soda-lime glass

Dimensions vary

Photo by Janice Peacock

After many years of doing flat glass, a demonstration by Nancy Tobey ignited my interest in lampworking. I have been lucky to learn from Nancy, Sally Prasch, Kristina Logan, and Heather Trimlett. The borosilicate color palette reminds me of aged Oriental carpets—hence the name.

JIMMY LOU JACKSON
Other Worlds, 2003

Lampworked; stringer; enamel; dichroic and soda-lime glass

3.8 x 2.5 cm

Photo by Terry Nelson

JAMES R. CASSADY, M.D.
Isfahan Garden Carpet, 2002

Lampworked; raked; stringer; frit; borosilicate glass

3 x 1 cm

Photo by Steve Gyurina

PATTI LEOTA GENACK
Spotted Pony, 2003

Lampworked; sculpted; reduction and
enamel frit; twistie; soda-lime glass

4.5 x 5.5 x 1.7 cm

Photo by Steve Gyurina

KATHY JOHNSON
The Black Stallion, 2003

Lampworked; handmade cane;
soda-lime glass

5.7 x 6 x 1.9 cm

Photo by Roger Schreiber

LILIANA CIRSTEA GLENN
New England Beaches, 2003

Lampworked; encased; stringer; partial silver fuming and reduction; silver foil; soda-lime glass

4.4 x 1.9 x .9 cm

Photo by Steve Gyurina

JINX GARZA
Nautilus, 2003

Lampworked; latticino; handmade murrina; stringer decoration; soda-lime glass

9 x 19 x 19 mm

Photo by Kathleen Tully

Many ancient cultures believed that eye beads were imbued with the power to ward off evil spirits and deflect the evil eye. This perspective on personal power has fascinated me, and evil eyes have become my trademark beads. I make my contemporary interpretations of these magical beads with my own intricate glass canes cut into slices to give the irises depth and detail. This particular cane reminds me of the spines inside a nautilus shell.

DEBBY YABCZANKA
Untitled, 2003

Flameworked; encased; plunged dots; soda-lime glass

1.7 x 1.3 cm

Photo by Jim Swallow

JODY LANE
Blue Moon Carmel Clusters, 2003

Lampworked; tube implosion; stringer;
borosilicate glass

3.8 x 2.5 x .6 cm

Photo by Chris Shutt

I generally have a plan when I sit down to work, but it's amazing that the glass just takes over and I get entirely different results.

DONNA NOVA
Spring Leaf Necklace, 2003

Lampworked; pressed leaves; goldstone; soda-lime glass; sterling silver clasp

2.5 x 2.5 x 50.8 cm (necklace)

Photo by artist

341

BRENDAN BLAKE
Cosmos Series, 2003

Lampworked; blown; marbled; borosilicate glass tubing

3 x 2 cm (left); 2.5 x 2 cm (right)

Photo by Shauna Blake

DIANA EAST
Aladdin's Palace and Mosque, 2002

Flameworked; gold fumed; enamel; sand-blasted; etched; dichroic and soda-lime glass

3.2 x 2.2 x .9 cm (each bead)

Photo by artist

343

Working on a mountaintop, I can't help being inspired by the natural beauty that flows (and in this case flies!) through our studio doors.

KIM WERTZ
Dragonflies and Butterfly, 2003

Lampworked; three-piece articulated beads; soda-lime glass; sterling wire with sterling accents

7.2 x 5.5 cm (largest bead)

Photo by Doc Damage

This necklace is designed to be
viewed not only from the front,
but from the back as well.

JENNIFER BROESKA
Green Scream, 2002

Lampworked; soda-lime glass;
sterling silver accents

15 x 12 x 2.5 cm

Photo by Ken Mayer

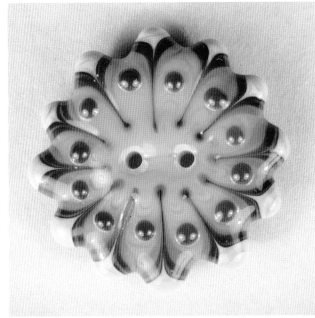

The colors in this button were inspired by a swimsuit I saw at the beach—people will wear things to the beach in color combos they would not be caught dead in elsewhere.

PATTI L. CAHILL
Spirograph Button (Swimsuit), 2003

Lampworked; dots; raked; soda-lime glass

3.8 x 3.8 x .9 cm

Photo by artist

JENNIFER PLACE
Patterned Bracelet, 2003

Flameworked; two-hole beads; soda-lime glass; seed bead accents

3.2 x 19 cm (bracelet)

Photo by artist

If you're too busy to play, you're too busy.

VER ET FRAMBOISE
Various Beads and Cabochons, 2001

Lampworked; murrini; soda-lime glass

3.3 cm (largest bead)

Photo by artist

347

LAURIE OLSON-SABOL
Hawaiian Flowers, 2003

Lampworked; trailed stringer; dots and
layered dots; plunged and raked;
soda-lime glass; pressed bead accents,
sterling silver accents and findings

61 cm (necklace)

Photo by artist

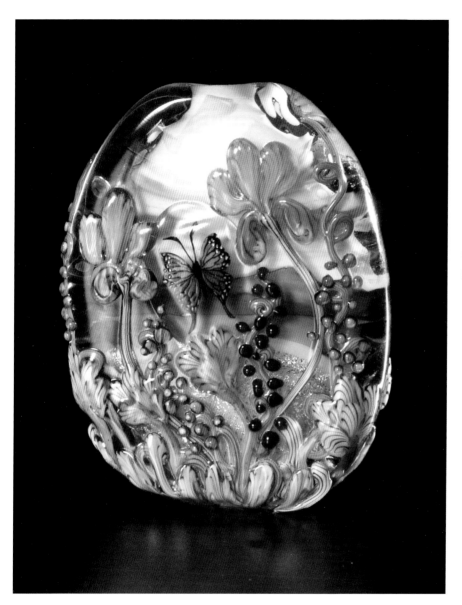

PATI WALTON
Butterfly Garden, 2003

Lampworked; encased; twistie;
handmade murrini; silver foil;
soda-lime glass

5 x 3.8 x 1.9 cm

Photo by Tomãs Del Amo

AMY CASWELL
Tigger the Cat, 2003

Lampworked; sculpted;
soda-lime glass

4.1 x 1.7 x 1.3 cm

Photo by Joseph Caswell

PEGGY ROSE
Rott in a Pot, 2003

Lampworked; sculpted;
soda-lime glass

3.5 x 2.2 x 2.2 cm

Photo by artist

CONNIE PAUL
Cats, I'm Shy!, 2003

Lampworked; sculpted; soda-lime
glass; sterling silver wire

4 x 2 x 1.8 cm (each bead)

Photo by Averill Lehan

351

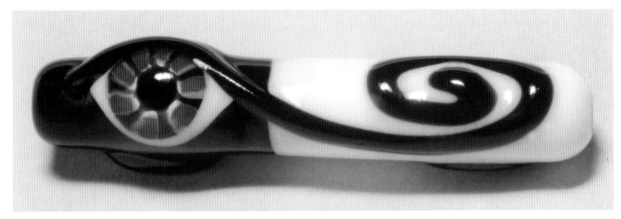

JINX GARZA
The Thrill of Victory,
2003

Lampworked; handmade
murrina; stringer decoration;
soda-lime glass

9 x 50 x 9 mm

Photo by Kathleen Tully

THOMAS JOHNSON
Untitled, 2003

Lampworked; bicone; marvered;
soda-lime glass

2.7 x 1.4 x 1.4 cm

Photo by artist

ICHIRO IKEMIYAGI
Kofu (Old Kimono Cloth), 2002

Lampworked; soda-lime glass

1.7 x 1.7 cm

Photo by artist

MELANIE LEWIS
Nutritious and Delicious, 2002

Flameworked; dot and stringer
techniques; soda-lime glass; seed
bead accents and sterling silver clasp

2.5 x 1 cm (largest bead)

Photo by George R. Campbell

LINDA CHAMBERS
Untitled, 2003

Flameworked; encased; pulled stringer;
filigrana; acid etched; soda-lime glass;
sterling silver accents

Dimensions vary

Photo by Kim Kauffman

I use unusual shapes and color combinations to evoke memories of tide pools, canyon striations, and even earthworms in my work. Applying multiple layers of color produces a rich texture that is deeply bedded under the smooth glass. My favorite comment about my work came from a client, who said there was such depth and movement that she would like to live inside one of my beads.

NANCY TOBEY
The Firestorms, 2003

Lampworked; raised dots; enamel; borosilicate glass

6.5 x 1 x 1 cm (largest bead)

Photo by Paul Avis

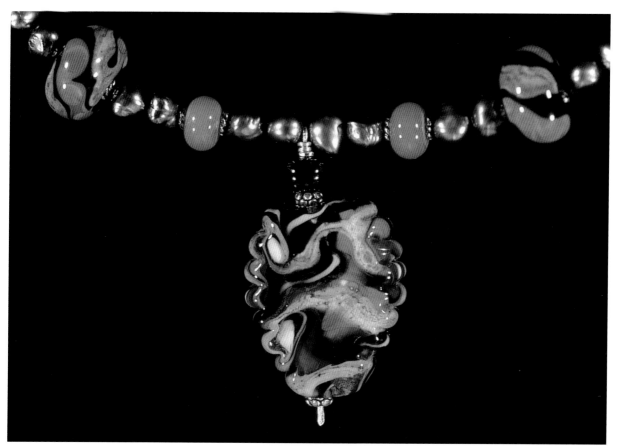

I'm a textile person who discovered glass a few years ago. I love playing with colors and shapes and seeing what the glass will do.

CATHY McNASSOR
Necklace, 2002

Lampworked; stringer; dots; soda-lime glass; pearl, pewter, and silver accents

50 cm (necklace); 3.8 x 2.9 x .9 cm (focal bead)

Photo by Dick Meier

357

JANICE PEACOCK
Aurora Necklace, 2002

Lampworked; fine silver foil; soda-lime glass;
sterling beads and stainless steel cable

45.7 cm (necklace); 5 x 2.5 cm (largest bead)

Photo by artist

There is nothing more exciting than opening your kiln to a new batch of beads and discovering that your color combination is dynamite!

JENNIFER BROESKA
Purple Passion, 2003

Lampworked; encased; dots; soda-lime glass; handmade sterling silver accents

Dimensions vary

Photo by Ken Mayer

LYNNE ELLIOTT
Pinwheel, 2003

Lampworked; layers of variegated dots; handmade ribbon cane; soda-lime glass

1.3 x 3.2 x 3.2 cm

Photo by David Orr

DEBBIE CROWLEY
Heart's Delight Perfume, 2003

Lampworked; sculpted; blown vessel; reduction powder; enamel; dichroic, soda-lime, and borosilicate glass; sterling silver and semi-precious stone accents

33 x 27.9 x 2.5 cm

Photo by Harold Wood

The mask may be considered a universal archetype—overused, in some critics' minds—but definitely not mine. We all need a friend to help watch out for us.

SAGE
Watcher/Mask, 1999

Lampworked; murrini; dots; feathered lines; soda-lime glass

4.4 x 3.1 x .9 cm

Photo by Tom Holland

YUMI TAJIKA
Okinawa, 2003

Lampworked; fused; handmade millefiori; layered; soda-lime glass

3.2 x 3.8 x 1 cm

Photo by artist

Layering on various colors and overheating
creates great special effects. Some
controlled, some surprises!

SHER BERMAN
Extreme Enamels, 2003

Flameworked; layered enamel powder;
goldstone stringer; overheated;
soda-lime glass

3.2 x 2.5 cm (vessel);
4.4 x 3.2 cm (largest bead)

Photo by Greg Kuepfer

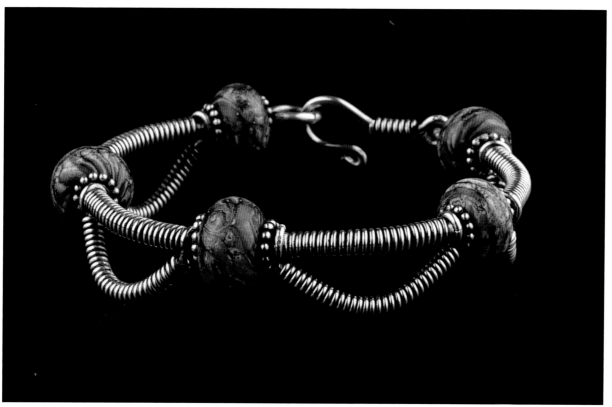

BETH BOAL
*Collaboration Bangle
(Coral Agate Series),* 2002

Lampworked; silver foil; soda-lime
glass; sterling silver wire

Wirework by Lori Merel

18.4 cm (bracelet);
15 x 9 mm (largest bead)

Photo by David Dale Photography

EMIKO NUMATA
Cat à la Carte, 2003

Lampworked; handmade
millefiori; lead glass

2.3 x 2 x 1.8 cm

Photo by MGM (JAPAN)

I love tea, teapots, the ritual of tea, and the sharing of teatime with a friend. My teapot beads honor the tradition of tea.

KARAN DOTSON
Round White Teapot, 2003

Flameworked; sculpted; soda-lime glass; handle of silver wire and seed beads, pewter and silver accents

3.2 x 2.5 x 1.9 cm

Photo by Robert Batey

These reproductions of actual fish species are my way of celebrating the wonders of our oceans.

PAMELA DUGGER
Panther Grouper, 2003

Lampworked; hollow; sculpted; encased; dots; soda-lime glass with borosilicate glass stand

7.6 x 3.8 x 10.2 cm

Photo by Jeffrey O'Dell

VER ET FRAMBOISE
Two Beads, 2003

Lampworked; murrini; soda-lime glass

2.1 x 2.3 cm (largest bead)

Photo by artist

This is one of those techniques you sort of stumble on. After I made these I was told it couldn't be done.

ADRIAN MENSTELL
Aurora Necklace, 2000

Lampworked; encased; reduction frit; silver; soda-lime glass; sterling silver spacers and accents

61 cm (necklace); 2.5 x 1.9 cm (focal bead)

Photo by Jerry Downs

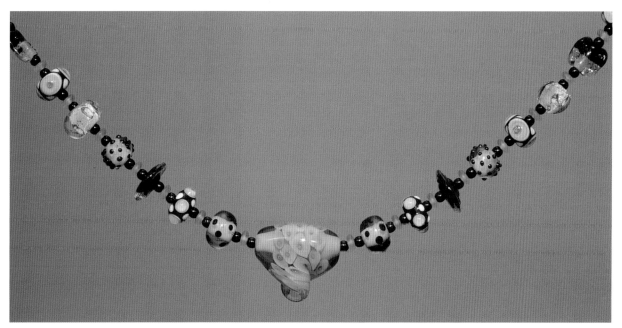

I like to manipulate molten glass and "freeze" flowing motion.

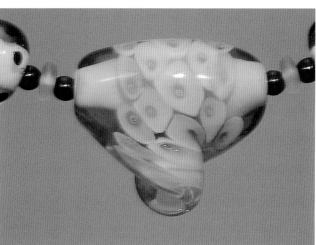

SUSAN MURRAY HEINE
A Twist of Lime, 2003

Lampworked; plunged and twisted dots; soda-lime glass; sterling silver findings

45.7 cm (necklace);
3 x 2.5 cm (focal bead)

Photo by Bill Sheets Photography,
Louisville, KY

369

I have found glass to be a limitless medium for expression, showing flexibility, sound sharpness, size, and movement. I was inspired to make a bead to show my idea of world peace.

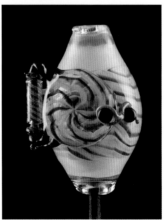

SALLY PRASCH
Open to Peace, 2002

Flameworked; sandblasted; hinged door; borosilicate glass

2.5 x 1.9 x 1.9 cm

Photo by Tommy Olof Elder

A positive affirmation is written on these beads. For me, these beads are my meditation as I focus on the affirmation. I believe the energy is passed along to the recipient of the bead.

MONA LINDSEY GOLLAN
Talisman I, 2003

Lampworked; encased; stringer; hand-pulled cane; silver foil; soda-lime glass

3.8 x 2.2 cm

Photo by artist

Working with leftover scraps of stained glass is something I feel strongly about. There is far too much of it landing in the garbage. It is precious and great fun to use.

KATE DREW-WILKINSON
Tide Pool in Sunlight, 2001

Lampworked; encased; cane; silver leaf; sheet glass remnants; silver and pearl accents

5 x 3.2 cm

Photo by Sandy Upson

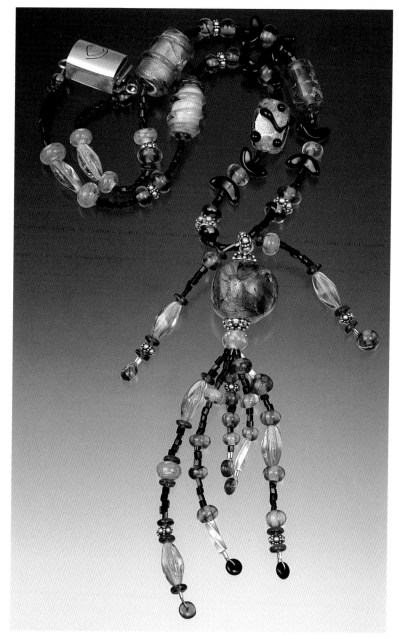

LINDA OSBORNE
Turquoise-Blue Sea Fantasy, 2002

Lampworked; gold foil; soda-lime glass; vintage jet accents and silver clasp

50.8 cm (necklace)

Photo by Steve Meltzer

MELANIE LEWIS
Primarily Fun, 2003

Flameworked; stacked dots and trailing
techniques; soda-lime glass; sterling
silver spacers and clasp

2 x 1.5 cm (largest bead)

Photo by George R. Campbell

ASHLEY WATSON
Do-Dads Bracelet, 2003

Lampworked; encased;
dots; latticino; soda-lime
glass; sterling silver
accents and findings

17.8 cm (bracelet);
1.3 x .5 cm (beads)

Photo by Josh Phillips

To give a special glow
to this hollow bead,
I etched the inside
surface of the glass.

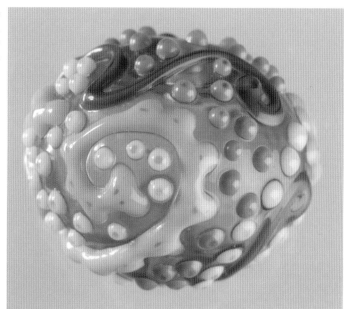

KIM VANANTWERP-POENISCH
Paisley Focal, 2003

Lampworked; hollow; surface
decoration of stringer and
dots; acid etched on inside;
soda-lime glass

2 x 2.5 cm

Photo by Michael Kellet

JANE PRAXEL
Vineyard, 2003

Lampworked; silver foil and
reduction frit; soda-lime glass

4.4 x 2 cm

Photo by David Orr

INARA KNIGHT
Flowers for Robert, 2002

Torchworked; dichroic inclusions; frit; trailing;
flattened; tooled; soda-lime glass

66 cm (necklace); 7 x 4.4 x .6 cm (focal bead)

Photo by Jeff O'Dell

LINDA CHAMBERS
Untitled, 2003

Flameworked; shaped; surface decoration
of stringer, dots, and raking; soda-lime
glass; sterling silver accents

Dimensions vary

Photo by Kim Kauffman

MARTHA GIBERSON
Ghost Trails, 2002

Flameworked; hollow; enamel;
soda-lime glass

61 x 3.8 cm (necklace)

Photo by Steve Gyurina

KATE ROTHRA
Ocean and Earth Series, 2003

Lampworked; stringer; dichroic and soda-lime glass; glass bead accents

66 cm (necklace)

Photo by George Post

BERNADETTE SCARANI MAHFOOD
Mardi Gras, 2002

Flameworked and kilnformed beads; soda-lime glass; handmade sterling silver chain

17.8 x 10.2 x 1.6 cm

Photo by Larry Sanders

JENNIFER LYNN STOWMAN
Misty Reflection, 2003

Lampworked; sterling silver leaf;
soda-lime glass

2.5 x 1.9 x 1.3 cm

Photo by artist

CHIEKO SASE
Mizu-no-tama, 2003

Lampworked; platinum foil; baking
soda; lead glass

2 x 2.4 x 2.3 cm

Photo by Hidetoshi Maki

CONNIE PAUL
Heartfelt, 2003

Lampworked; silver foil; soda-lime
glass; sterling silver findings

2.8 cm (focal bead)

Photo by Averill Lehan

GENEVIÈVE MARTINEAU
Aboriginal Bead, 2003

Lampworked; dots; stringer; soda-lime glass

3.8 x 1.3 x 1.3 cm

Photo by Steve Gyurina

This is the end view of a bead with a seamless mosaic design comprising six murrini, including hollow end caps. The design of the adjacent murrini flows together.

JAMES ALLEN JONES
Mosaic Glass Bead, 2003

Lampworked; handmade murrini; soda-lime glass

2.5 x 1.9 cm

Photo by artist

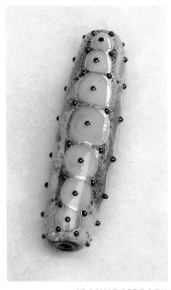

JOANNE MORASH
Chrysalis, 2002

Lampworked; silver fuming;
silver foil; soda-lime glass

7 x 2 cm

Photo by *Bead & Button*

AKIHIRO OHKAMA
Flower in the Water (Lily), 2002

Lampworked; murrini; silver powder;
soda-lime glass

2.5 x 2 x 2 cm

Photo by Youichi Sueyoshi

The bear is a symbol for strength,
endurance, and healing.

CHAD PITTS
Strength-Bear Totem, 2003

Blown; inside-out technique; precious metals;
reduced and shaped; borosilicate glass

2.5 x 6.4 x 1.3 cm

Photo by artist

JENNY NEWTSON
Sputnik Long #20, 2003

Lampworked; stacked dots; mixed colors; soda-lime glass; sterling silver and crystal accents

71.1 cm (necklace);
2.5 x 2.9 x 2.5 cm (focal bead)

Photo by Daniel Van Rossen

RENÉ ROBERTS
Nebula Black Necklace, 2003

Flameworked; blown glass shards; metal
leaf (fine silver and 24k gold); soda-lime
glass; 14k gold, sterling silver, patinaed
copper, and rubber components

45.7 cm (necklace); 5 cm (focal bead)

Photo by Hap Sakwa

LISA WALSH
Three Complex Stars, 2000

Flameworked; dots and raked
dots; soda-lime glass

3.8 x 3.8 cm

Photo by John Yen

BARBARA BECKER SIMON
Fish Bead, 2003

Lampworked; dots; stringers;
dichroic and soda-lime glass

5 x 4.4 x 1.3 cm

Photo by Rob Stegmann

MICHEALE GORDON
Textured Bead Pendant, 2003

Flameworked; encased; plunged; raised dots; handmade cane; goldstone; soda-lime glass; sterling silver findings, pearl and crystal accents

3 x 2 x 1.5 cm

Photo by Kevin McHone

MITRA TOTTEN
Raised Floral Focal Bead, 2003

Lampworked; layered; raised dots; soda-lime glass

2.5 x 1.6 cm

Photo by artist

CANDY M. GRAMMEL
Just Glass and Gold, 2003

Kiln-fused; layered; 24k-gold
decal; fusible glass

3.25 x 2 x .75 cm

Photo by Brian Lickliter, Heritage Studios

I particularly enjoy
working with greens and
blues; the colors often
lend a soothing natural
feel to the piece.

D. STEPHEN GREENWAY
Millefiori Arboretum, 2003

Lampworked; millefiori;
soda-lime glass

1.2 x 2.3 cm

Photo by Kate Baldwin

SABRINA PIERSON
Adornment, 2003

Lampworked; encased; various surface decorations; metal oxides; soda-lime glass; amethyst and seed bead accents, sterling silver clasp

261.6 cm (necklace); 5 x 8 x 10 mm (beads)

Photo by Kate Baldwin

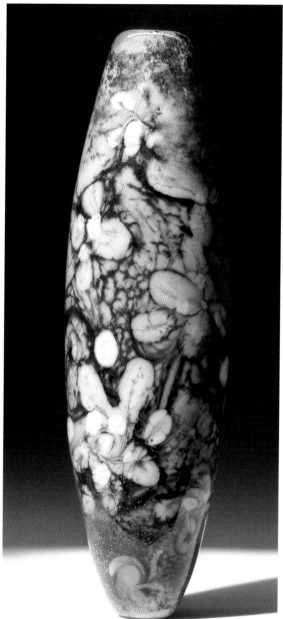

MAVIS SMITH
Fairy Queen, 2003

Lampworked; twisted stringer; handmade encased murrini; soda-lime glass; sterling silver wire and findings; crystal accents

2.5 x 1.9 x 1.3 cm

Photo by artist

DIANA DUGINA
Batik Bleue, 2003

Lampworked; ribbon cane; boiled enamel; soda-lime glass

5 x 1.6 x 1.6 cm

Photo by Steve Gyurina

Masking is a fairly technical process—creating negative space on the bead's surface and then using that negative space to create more negative space and patterns. Wow…did I really write that?

NANCY LAWLER
Masked Beads, 2003

Flameworked; layered and masked dots; soda-lime glass; 14k gold vermeil beads and clasp

Necklace by Susan Beresford

45.7 cm (necklace); 4 cm (largest bead)

Photo by artist

DARLENE DURRWACHTER RUSHING
Coral Visions, 2002

Flameworked; silver fumed; twistie;
soda-lime glass; agate and silver accents

2.5 x 1.3 x 1.9 cm (largest bead)

Photo by David L. Smith

LINDA NICHOLSON
Poppy Pod, 2002

Flameworked; sculpted; stringer; reduction frit;
goldstone; soda-lime glass; silver accents

7.6 x 2.9 x 2.9 cm

Photo by artist

MITRA TOTTEN
Encased Floral Vessel Pendant, 2003

Lampworked; encased; soda-lime glass;
removable cork stopper

5.7 x 1.9 cm

Photo by artist

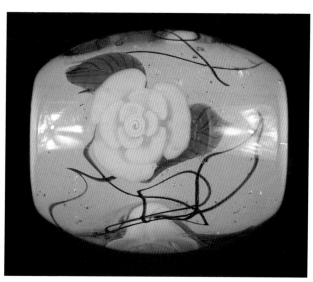

AKIHIRO OHKAMA
Rose, 2003

Lampworked; murrini; soda-lime glass

2.5 x 2 x 2 cm

Photo by Youichi Sueyoshi

I'm fascinated by the properties of glass—the reflection of light, the fluidity. My recent work is of larger constructions, more dramatic statements, but with simpler beads—here, the drip.

DARLENE DURRWACHTER RUSHING
Because the Night...., 2002

Flameworked; dichroic and soda-lime glass; vintage crystal and sterling silver accents

7.6 x 1.3 x .6 cm (largest bead)

Photo by David L. Smith

BRUCE ST. JOHN MAHER
Optics, 2001

Fused; coldworked; dichroic and fusible glass

2.5 cm

Photo by Robert K. Liu

COVER ARTIST

Kristina Logan is an independent artist who lives and works in Portsmouth, New Hampshire and Provence, France. Kristina writes that beads "are part of my lifelong fascination with art and ornamentation. Glass beads form a historical thread, connecting people and cultures throughout our history. I am passionate about my work and about teaching others." She is widely published and travels extensively throughout the United States and Europe, teaching workshops and lecturing on contemporary glass beads and jewelry.

INDEX

Amy Trescott Bellevue, Washington
Pages 79, 168

Heather Trimlett El Cajon, California
Pages 34, 80

Toshiki Uchida Saitama ken, Japan
Pages 154, 189, 205

Kim VanAntwerp-Poenisch College Station, Texas
Pages 216, 375

Karen Kay Velarde Newport, Virginia
Pages 275, 280

Patricia Zabreski Venaleck Macomb, Michigan
Pages 149, 249

VER ET FRAMBOISE (Nicole Zumkeller and Eric Seydoux), Vaulruz, Switzerland
Pages 144, 347, 367

Reijiro Wada Kanagawa, Japan
Page 204

Michelle Waldren Eagle River, Alaska
Pages 79, 82, 208

Caryn Walsh Apache Junction, Arizona
Page 254

Lisa Walsh Lafayette, Indiana
Page 390

Pati Walton Larkspur, Colorado
Page 349

Vickie Warburton Springdale, Arkansas
Page 246

Kathryn Wardill South Yarra, Melbourne, Australia
Pages 182, 248

Ashley Watson Lexington, Kentucky
Pages 50, 375

Catharine Weaver Sitka, Alaska
Page 180

Debby Weaver Middletown, Maryland
Pages 18

Debra K. Wells Evergreen, Colorado
Page 278

Kim Wertz Kneeland, California
Pages 173, 302, 344

Patti Wood Whiteley Lawrenceville, New Jersey
Page 289

Faith Wickey Centreville, Michigan
Pages 161, 217

Beth Williams Gloucester, Massachusetts
Pages 49, 54, 139

Michelle Wilman Calgary, Alberta, Canada
Page 264

John Winter Potomac, Maryland
Pages 192, 294

Karen Wojcinski Dunkirk, New York
Page 148

Pamela Kay Wolfersberger Lewis Center, Ohio
Pages 51, 218

Karen Wolffis Portage, Michigan
Page 202

Barbara A. Wright Trinidad, California
Pages 26, 206

Julie Wuest San Mateo, California
Page 224

Debby Yabczanka St. Petersburg, Florida
Page 339

April Zilber Berkeley, California
Pages 134, 334

Lea Zinke Clearwater, Florida
Page 124

Jen Zitkov Corning, New York
Pages 58, 276

ACKNOWLEDGMENTS

My heartfelt thanks to the beadmakers from around the globe who submitted exciting and innovative work for this publication. I am impressed with the diversity of form and depth of expression achieved in your work.

Juror Cathy Finegan is a passionate advocate of the art form. She addressed the selection process with good humor, integrity, enthusiasm, and intelligence. I was impressed with her thoughtful approach to the work.

A devoted team at Lark Books was responsible for the production of this volume. Editorial Assistants Annie Wolff Hollyfield and Rebecca Lim were indispensable in gathering the text and the images. Associate Art Editor Shannon Yokeley provided much needed technical expertise. And Art Director Stacey Budge has a genuine enthusiasm for glass beads, which is certainly evident in her inspired design. Thank you to all.

CONVERSION CHART

10 mm = 1 cm
6 mm = ¼ in
1.3 cm = ½ in
1.9 cm = ¾ in
2.5 cm = 1 in

Ichiro Ikemiyagi, *Scroll,* 2003. Photo by artist